ELECTING A CONSTITUTION

STUDIES IN ILLINOIS CONSTITUTION MAKING
Joseph P. Pisciotte, *Editor*

Other titles in the series:

CONSTITUTION MAKING IN ILLINOIS, 1818-1970
JANET CORNELIUS

FOR THE FIRST HOURS OF TOMORROW
The New Illinois Bill of Rights
ELMER GERTZ

LOBBYING AT THE
ILLINOIS CONSTITUTIONAL CONVENTION
IAN D. BURMAN

TO JUDGE WITH JUSTICE
History and Politics of Illinois Judicial Reform
RUBIN G. COHN

BALLOTS FOR CHANGE
New Suffrage and Amending Articles for Illinois
ALAN S. GRATCH and VIRGINIA H. UBIK

POLITICS OF THE PURSE
Revenue and Finance in the
Sixth Illinois Constitutional Convention
JOYCE D. FISHBANE and GLENN W. FISHER

A FUNDAMENTAL GOAL
Education for the People of Illinois
JANE GALLOWAY BURESH

ROLL CALL!
Patterns of Voting in the
Sixth Illinois Constitutional Convention
DAVID KENNEY, JACK R. VAN DER SLIK, and SAMUEL J. PERNACCIARO

All books in the series are in paperback @ $3.45 each.

Electing a Constitution: The Illinois Citizen and the 1970 Constitution

JOANNA M. WATSON

7 2280 P

Published for the
INSTITUTE OF GOVERNMENT AND PUBLIC AFFAIRS
by the
UNIVERSITY OF ILLINOIS PRESS
Urbana   Chicago   London

*Special appreciation is expressed to
the Field Foundation of Illinois,
whose financial support has made
this series possible.*

LIBRARY OF CONGRESS CATALOGING IN PUBLICATION DATA

Watson, JoAnna M
    Electing a constitution.

    (Studies in Illinois constitution making)
    Includes index.
    1. Illinois. Constitutional Convention, 1969–1970.
    2. Illinois—Constitutional history. I. Illinois.
University at Urbana-Champaign. Institute of Government
and Public Affairs. II. Title. III. Series.
KF116011970.A29   342'.773'024   79-26224
ISBN 0-252-00458-2 pbk.

To Shand and Mark

Contents

Foreword   ix

Preface   xi

I.   The Voters and Constitutional Elections   3

II.   A Convention Call is Prepared   8

III.   The Campaign for Con Con Goes to the People   23

IV.   Con Con Election Analysis   36

V.   Election of Convention Delegates   43

VI.   The Ballot Battle   64

VII.   Campaign for the "Main Package"   71

VIII. The Mini-Campaigns   87

IX.   Analysis of the Vote at the Ratifying Election   99

Appendix A: Vote for Calling a Constitutional Convention   116

Appendix B: Primary Election for Members of Con Con   118

Appendix C: General Election for Members of Con Con   122

Appendix D: Special Election for Proposed Constitution   132

Index   135

Foreword

The Sixth Illinois Constitutional Convention held in 1970 has provided a wealth of material for researchers interested in studying the constitutional revision process. To aid students of this process, as well as practitioners, the Institute of Government and Public Affairs has authorized the writing and publication of a series of monographs, *Studies in Illinois Constitution Making*. Each volume in the series examines an aspect of the Illinois convention and attempts to deal with some of the questions that have been raised about state constitutional revision. All of the authors were involved to some degree with the convention itself. The methodology of analysis and the conclusions drawn by each study are as varied as are the individual authors and their relationship to the convention.

In this monograph Ms. Watson researches in depth a subject only briefly considered by other authors in the series: the several elections that produced (1) the convention call, (2) the selection of convention delegates and (3) ratification of the constitution. These elections were a fundamental ingredient for a successful convention and a study of the process through which they evolved is a valuable contribution to this series. Together with the other monographs in the series it increases our understanding of the various phases necessary for a successful constitutional revision. The series as a whole provides valuable insight into the dedication and hard work put forth by the delegates in the effort to produce a document that was both serviceable and acceptable to the citizens of Illinois.

The Institute expresses its deep appreciation to the Field Foundation of Illinois which recognized the need for these studies and provided the funding for them. As in each of the studies the statements and views expressed in this monograph are solely the responsibility of the author.

Joseph P. Pisciotte Samuel K. Gove
Series Editor *Institute Director*

Preface

I became personally involved in the Illinois constitutional revision process in the autumn of 1969. For the Champaign-Urbana News Gazette, I doggedly tailed the contenders for the two 48th district seats in the constitutional convention. In the capacity of part-time staff to the Local Government Committee of the Convention, I was able to secure a place from which to observe the nascent constitutional process and prepare for my role as recorder of the ratification process. The materials from which I drew my description and analyses of the constitutional convention call in 1968 had been collected by Joseph Pisciotte. His own article, "How Illinois Did It" in the *National Civic Review* (July 1969), was my introduction to that election. In addition, the Institute of Government and Public Affairs at the University of Illinois maintained an extensive newspaper and documents file on the subject.

My experience as participant-observer in the ratification campaign provided a rare opportunity to witness firsthand the activities at the campaign headquarters of the Illinois Citizens for a New Constitution (ICNC), the citizen-based campaigns for the reform options of the separately submitted issues of legislative representation and judicial selection, and the self-styled ratification campaigns of several Chicago and downstate delegates. I sat through the late November public hearings of the Democratic party on the proposed constitution and fretted over the possibility that Mayor Daley would not endorse the document—and rejoiced when he did! After all, I knew I was going to set all this down on paper and I naturally preferred to present a tale of constitutional revision success.

On election eve I took the elevator up to ICNC headquarters and settled down with the others to watch the returns as the people of Illinois elected their new constitution.

* * *

In the course of writing the story behind the success that unfolded that evening, I had a great deal of guidance and good counsel from friends and colleagues too numerous to mention here. I do, however, wish to thank a number of specific people for their special help. For their careful review and editorial wizardry, I thank Elizabeth Stewart, Harriet Imrey, Helen Thursh, and, especially, Anna Merritt. I wish to thank, as well, Mabel Edmiston, Lorena McClain, and Florence Edmison for typing and retyping the manuscript, which is a tedious but critical task. And last, I want to express my special sense of gratitude to Ashley Nugent for building such excellent files on the constitutional campaigns.

ELECTING A CONSTITUTION

I

The Voters and
Constitutional Elections

> To most voters, constitutional revision is a highly eso-
> teric subject, involving hazy abstractions that appear to
> have little direct relation to their personal affairs.
>
> Albert Sturm

On December 15, 1970, at a special election, Illinois voters approved a new state constitution, a feat that had eluded many other
states. This was the last of four elections in which the people of Illinois had the opportunity to participate in constitutional revision:
the first had been the call for a constitutional convention, popularly
referred to as Con Con; it was overwhelmingly approved at the
November 1968 general election. Delegates to the convention were
then selected in two separate elections: a primary on September 23,
1969 and a general election on November 18, 1969.

A number of factors contributed to this successful election story.
These include, first of all, the persistent efforts of a small number of
reform-minded individuals whose first involvement dated back to
the formation of the Committee on Constitutional Revision of the
Chicago Bar Association in the late 1940s and who began the early
preparations of this endeavor. Second, a reservoir of support had
developed for the so-called blue ballot used since 1950 in submitting
constitutional propositions to the voters. Because of its initial
success, it had become associated in the minds of many voters with

3

"good government."[1] This support would provide the ready base upon which to build an electoral majority.

A third factor contributing to the ultimate successful passage of the constitution was a pragmatic understanding of the political map of Illinois by those whose task it was to wage a successful campaign for adoption. About half of the state's eleven million people live in Cook County (Chicago). The rest of the population is scattered in the 101 counties in the so-called downstate area. This division produces an electoral seesaw of sorts in which success or defeat depends upon the relative support each division generates at election time. Overwhelming opposition by either division, as with the nearly twenty-to-one negative vote returned by Cook County against the proposed 1922 Illinois constitution, can be decisive. Consequently, a careful balance of electoral forces is the critical first step in a successful election strategy. Only compromise can break down the divisions created by disparate political, economic, and regional interests; this political reality clearly conditioned decisions during both the convention and the campaign. As convention President Samuel Witwer stated some years later:

> While the new constitution may not be the model document that some political reformers had hoped it would be, I think that we produced the best document that could be adopted in this politically diverse state.[2]

In the election for ratification of the 1970 constitution, it was the eleventh-hour endorsement of the proposed document by the Cook County Democratic party that actually tipped the balance in favor of adoption. However, the balance itself had been struck by the fourth critical variable of the success story—the convention delegates. Seeds of good will and public approval were sown by the delegates' conscientious efforts during the constitution drafting stage. This early public support was then nourished by hard and highly personal campaigns by most delegates in their own and neighboring districts.

This activist effort on the part of the delegates was the decentralized portion of what was an otherwise centralized campaign for adoption, and presents another interesting issue in the area of constitutional revision: should there be a high level of voter participation and how actively should such participation be sought? The cen-

[1] Taped interview with Samuel Witwer, winter 1968.

[2] Samuel Witwer, "Preface Symposium: the 1970 Illinois Constitution," *John Marshall Journal of Practice and Procedure*, 11, no. 2 (winter 1977–78): 254.

tral campaign committee, with headquarters in Chicago, pursued what it believed to be the correct formula for success: a low-keyed, nonconfrontation strategy. It too played an important role in the adoption of the 1970 constitution. However, the active campaign strategy of most delegates was in contrast to the seemingly passive one of the central committee. The committee was dismayed over what it considered overzealous and potentially troublesome activities by convention delegates on the campaign trail. Delegates were accused of having injected revenue matters into the campaign debate so much so that the central committee, against its own survey research recommendations, published an ad hoc brochure which attempted to allay voters' fears of increased taxes and runaway public spending. Delegates, in turn, bemoaned the lackluster style of campaign headquarters and were critical of its non-aggressiveness and "paper-pushing" mentality. In fact, both campaigns were important elements, for each sought to pull a different constituency onto the bandwagon. While delegates tried to woo voters back home, campaign headquarters sought to hold onto pre-existing statewide organizational support. By avoiding a comparison of the 1870 constitution and the proposed constitution in general, and by avoiding specific controversial issues, the committee maintained its loyal base of support while not stirring the opposition unnecessarily.

Studies of referenda campaigns frequently point to at least one important characteristic: the lower the turnout at the polls, the greater the chance for passage of the ballot question. Thus, the central campaign committee's ratification plan for the Illinois constitution at a special election incorporated the minimal turnout strategy. In fact, little more than a third of the Illinois electorate voted at the ratification election. Low turnout is not unusual: Albert Sturm, writing for the National Municipal League, has stated, "The generally low level of public interest reflected in nonvoting on constitutional issues exists in practically all states."[3] Observers of state government readily admit that the relationship between theoretical consensual politics and state constitutions is tenuous, if not actually nonexistent. It would appear that existing state constitutions are less the fruits of consensualism than of practical politics. On balance, this results as much from the realities of political life as from any formal strategic design. The problem of developing a constitutional consensus on the state level is twofold. First, few people take an

[3] Albert L. Sturm, *Thirty Years of State Constitution-Making, 1938–1968*, (New York: National Municipal League, 1970), p. 87.

active interest in constitution making. At those stages in the process in which voters may directly influence the nature and course of constitutional revision, only about 30 percent exercise the electoral prerogative. Voter turnout at special elections for constitutional revision in recent years has ranged from 19 percent in Rhode Island in 1968 to 46 percent in Maryland the same year. Needless to say, such limited voting activity drops far short not only of an electoral consensus but of a majority as well. Second, the problem of a small turnout of voters at constitutional elections is compounded by the fact that major socioeconomic segments of our society are conspicuously absent from the voter ranks.[4] Clearly then, voting on state constitutions does not approach the ideal of consensual theory.

The nature and form of an election certainly influence levels of voter participation. Quadrennial presidential elections unquestionably attract greatest voter activity. Off-year elections draw fewer participants—approximately one-third less. Local elections, when not dovetailed into the national electoral machinery, generally evidence least voter participation. Special elections, which are by definition outside the electoral routine, suffer accordingly. Special awareness campaigns must stimulate interest in an already "ballot-shocked" electorate. Surveys in Illinois just prior to the 1969 election for convention delegates and the 1970 election for constitutional ratification showed that a significant percentage of registered voters had no knowledge of these impending electoral events. The fact that an average of only 25 to 30 percent of voters in each county actually voted in these elections suffices to demonstrate the disinterest in special elections on the part of most voters.

More important than the effect of election devices and campaign strategies on voter behavior is the nature of the electoral issue and its inherent ability or inability to generate popular appeal. In this case, the issue is a constitution. By definition a constitution must meet two criteria: its principles not only must respond to the perceived common good, but they must withstand the test of time. *"A constitution,"* affirms Justice Cardozo, "states or ought to state not rules for the passing hour, but principles for an expanding future."[5] For many, a new constitution is an alien electoral issue, not simply because it is an issue seldom voted upon but because its futuristic/public-oriented framework is not a foreseeable part of their daily lives.

[4]V.O. Key, Jr., *Politics, Parties, and Pressure Groups* (New York: Thomas Y. Crowell Co., 1964), p. 642.

[5]Benjamin N. Cardozo, *The Nature of the Judicial Process* (New Haven: Yale University Press, 1948), p. 83.

Some issues are better suited than others to generate voter interest and participation in elections. Voters are attracted to candidates and then issues which are both relevant and relatively simple to understand. The issue of a constitution is neither relevant in any immediate way nor simple to understand. Furthermore the choice for many voters is not clear. Most understand as little about the existing constitution as about its proposed replacement. Many voters are not attracted to the very issue which most requires their endorsement. If constitutional governments derive their "just powers from the consent of the governed," a principle formally expressed in many state constitutions—including the 1870 Illinois constitution—then the electoral response should reflect substantial consent on this basic law. But if only a small portion of voters participates at elections to ratify the constitution, what can be said of that consensus from which flows governmental stability? Perhaps the answer lies not in the rate of voter turnout, but in the opportunity to vote.[6] Those voters who took advantage of the relatively rare opportunity to participate in constitutional revision and who recorded their position on the proposed constitution secured the legitimacy of the document and created a foundation for its effectiveness.

[6]Murray Edelman, *The Symbolic Uses of Politics* (Urbana: University of Illinois Press, 1964).

II

A Convention Call is Prepared

> . . . that the first order of business concerning constitu-
> tional amendments be the question of a constitutional
> convention. . . .
>
> Constitution Study Commission

The Gateway amendment campaign of 1950 set an organizational and strategic style that was subsequently utilized in a series of constitutional referenda, including the campaign for a constitutional convention that culminated in the 1970 referendum for ratification of the 1970 Illinois charter. This consistency of campaign style was guaranteed by a number of dedicated individuals whose efforts contributed to the major blue ballot endeavors between 1950 and 1969. Deviation from the original formula was attributable to the occasional input of new blood. The basic strategic format remained unchanged despite the fact that it proved unsuccessful more often than not. From 1952 to 1966, fifteen amendments were submitted to the voters and only six were approved, the last in 1966. Only two of those adopted were very far reaching—the 1954 reapportionment amendment and the 1962 judicial amendment. Three attempts to amend the revenue article were unsuccessful.[1]

A number of names appear over and over again among lists of amendment campaigners. For example, Samuel Witwer, the Chicago attorney who served as president of the constitutional con-

---

[1]Thomas R. Kitsos, "Constitutional Amendments and the Voter, 1952–1966," Commission Papers of the Institute of Government and Public Affairs, University of Illinois (Urbana, 1968), p. 5.

vention, figured heavily in both the Gateway (1950) and the legislative reapportionment (1954) amendment campaigns and was instrumental in creating the machinery for the 1968 convention call campaign. Richard Lockhart, editor of the *Illinois Political Reporter* and campaign manager for both the reapportionment and judicial amendment campaigns, was a major figure in both the 1968 convention call and 1970 ratification campaigns. William Allen, publications director of the Illinois Agricultural Association, had led organized opposition to the revenue article amendment campaign (1966) and acted as director of both the 1968 convention call and the 1970 ratification campaigns. And finally, the names of many loyal behind-the-scenes workers in previous amendment campaigns reappear among early endorsers and organizers of the effort for constitutional revision as members of the Constitution Study Commission, campaign organization committees, and other groups discussed in the following pages.

Recruitment of campaign chairmen has traditionally been a gubernatorial function. Cochairmen were typically a Chicago businessman and a downstate representative—presidents of the Illinois Agricultural Association were a popular gubernatorial choice. These kinds of decisions acknowledged the basic dichotomy in Illinois politics between Cook County, where half of the state's 11 million people reside, and downstate. In each campaign the Illinois Committee for Constitutional Revision (ICCR) was reactivated as a centralized citizen's campaign headquarters. Its major functions were to seek organizational endorsements and support, distribute materials, and solicit campaign contributions. However, the principal tasks of informing and politically activating voters fell to sympathetic organizations whose prime targets then became their own members. The 1967–68 campaign organizers, with a history of amendment ventures upon which to rely for guidance, obviously adopted much that had been tested in past campaigns. At the same time, they attempted to avoid the mistakes of the past, specifically the disastrous "yes" vote instruction on the 1958 judicial reform ballot, when some voters took the campaign instruction to mark "yes" on their blue ballots literally; since an "X" was the only acceptable ballot entry, writing "yes" had the effect of spoiling the ballot. So close was the vote that backers of the reform filed suit claiming that the proposal had actually received a popular majority. The suit was taken to the Illinois Supreme Court in hopes of obtaining a ruling that votes cast by voters who simply wrote the word "yes" rather than marking their ballots "X" should have been counted. The claim was rejected by the court two years later.[2]

HISTORY OF THE CONVENTION CALL REFERENDUM

The recommendations of the Constitution Study Commission, created by the 74th General Assembly in 1965 and chaired by Representative Marjorie Pebworth, a Republican from Riverdale and former president of the Illinois League of Women Voters, prefaced the effort to establish the machinery from which major constitutional revision would hopefully emanate. The very fact that the Constitution Study Commission existed was politically significant. In 1965 the Illinois House of Representatives was elected on an at-large basis. This was because the legislature and the executive had failed to agree on legislative reapportionment, so that the provision for at-large elections in case of such failure, contained in the 1954 constitutional amendment, was invoked. The result was a great infusion of new faces in the legislature, including many who were committed to reform. One of the actions of that legislature was to pass a bill creating the Constitution Study Commission.

In a unanimous report to the legislature, in 1967, the commission,[3] representing both political and geographic distinctions in the state, offered three recommendations:

1. that the Seventy-Fifth Illinois General Assembly place on the ballot for November, 1968, the question of calling a constitutional convention;

2. that the first order of busines concerning constitutional amendments be the question of a constitutional convention and that if the resolution for a constitutional convention is adopted by the requisite two-thirds majority in the House and Senate, then no further amendments be submitted to the electorate at the November, 1968, election; and

3. that the General Assembly continue the Constitution Study Commission, with an appropriation sufficient to support continued study and the preparation of background material for delegates to a convention.[4]

[2]Schribner v. Sachs, 18 Ill. 2nd 400 (1960).

[3]Commission membership included: *Senators*—David Davis, Alan Dixon, John Gilbert, Thomas Lyons (vice-chairman), Robert McCarthy, and Arthur Sprague. *Representatives*—Terrell Clarke, Francis Mahoney, John McNichols, Marjorie Pebworth (Chairman), Harris Rowe, and Edward Warman. *Public Members*—Louis Ancel (Secretary), Mrs. Henry Connor, Jordan Hillman, James Otis, Elbert Smith, Samuel Witwer. (William Stiehl filled the vacancy caused by the death of Mrs. Connor in October 1966).

[4]Report of the State of Illinois Constitution Study Commission, February 1967, p. 3.

The commission rejected lesser alternatives to constitutional revision, (i.e., the piecemeal or article-by-article approach) arguing that the electoral hurdles were practically insurmountable. Unlike constitutional amendments, the revised constitution proposed by a constitutional convention could be submitted to voters at a special election. It was the consensus of the commission that amendments traditionally failed because they were buried in a general election requiring many other decisions by the voters. The report noted that, although most amendments fail to receive support by a majority of those voting *at the election*, they are commonly favored by a majority voting *on the question*. Of twenty attempts to win approval of constitutional propositions at general elections since 1934, including the constitutional convention call of that year, nineteen were favored by a substantial majority of those who voted on the question. The voter participation rate on constitutional propositions at general elections was often as low as 40 percent prior to 1950, but averaged approximately 76 percent for questions submitted on the blue ballot between 1952 and 1966.[5]

Special elections are an obvious device for reducing the crippling numbers of "back-handed" negative votes created by lack of voter interest in otherwise candidate-oriented elections. However, the call for a constitutional convention could not enjoy the advantages of a special election and had to be placed, at legislative discretion, on a ballot in the forthcoming general election. Although the 1950 Gateway amendment had relaxed the requirements for passing amendments, a constitutional convention call was exempted and still required approval by a majority of those voting in a general election. Since the convention call referendum was going to be conducted together with a presidential election that would bring out unusually large numbers of voters, both high voter participation rates and high approval rates would be required.

Given these constitutional requirements, identical joint resolutions were introduced in the spring session of the 76th General Assembly to authorize submission of the constitutional convention question at the November 5, 1968, election. Governor Otto Kerner strongly urged support for a constitutional convention in his State of the State message to the General Assembly on January 5, 1967. Despite heated debate, Senate Joint Resolution 2 was approved in the Senate by a vote of 50 to 0 and in the House by 150–14. It is be-

[5]Janet Cornelius, "A History of Constitution Making in Illinois," Commission Papers of the Institute of Government and Public Affairs, University of Illinois (Urbana, 1968), p. 114. See also, Kitsos, "Constitutional Amendments," p. 13.

lieved by some that the death of Mrs. Pebworth, chairman of the sponsoring commission, moved a number of legislators to vote for adoption of the convention resolution as a tribute to her.[6] Furthermore, many members who were otherwise opposed to constitutional reform were probably willing to vote for the measure because they felt its chances for popular approval were slim. Approval of the convention call would require "yes" votes by a majority of those voting at the election, and the Constitution Study Commission report had clearly defined the problem of historic voter nonparticipation on constitutional issues.

The protests outlined on the House floor against Resolution 2, foreshadowed the arguments convention proponents would encounter throughout much of the early campaign for public approval of the constitutional convention. These arguments hinged upon the method of selection of delegates to the convention and the fact that their manner of election would necessarily shape the style and final product of the convention. The 1870 constitution required that delegates be selected in the "same place and manner" as senators to the General Assembly. Thus it appeared that two delegates would be chosen from each senatorial district in the state on a partisan electoral basis. In oppposing this move, Representative John W. Lewis, formerly House Speaker and Secretary of State for Illinois, argued, for example, that because Cook County comprised thirty of the state's fifty-eight senatorial districts, the sixty delegates from that one particular county would hold the majority at the convention and would be able to dominate proceedings. "There is a basic difference in thinking between Cook and downstate," he emphasized, claiming that the imposition of one upon the other in constitutional matters was "dangerous."[7] (The record of voting at the convention, however, disproved the notion of Cook County unanimity.)

The Republican legislator was joined in his doubts about delegate selection by Thomas Hanahan, a Democrat and labor union official, whose fears echoed labor's opposition to the convention call: "As long as those 58 districts turn down minimum wage and other

[6] Undated memo from Peggy Norton, executive secretary of the Illinois Committee for a Constitutional Convention, p. 1. Alice B. Ihrig, taped interview, November 1968. "Constitutional Convention Clears Legislature," *Illinois Voter* 47, no. 5 (July–August, 1967): 1.

[7] Jane Tufford, "Constitutional Conventions in Illinois with Special Emphasis on the Fifth Convention and the Prospect for a Sixth" (M.A. Thesis, University of Illinois, May 1968), p. 80.

progressive legislation, I don't think anything good can come out of a constitutional convention."[8]

Despite these criticisms, the convention call received early organizational and editorial support. Almost immediately after the end of the legislative session, an informal group of civic activists formed to lay the groundwork for the upcoming referendum campaign. This group was spearheaded by members of the League of Women Voters and Chicago Bar Association, long-time agitators for constitutional revision. Attending the first luncheon meeting at this embryonic stage in development of a citizen's campaign for the convention were six representatives of the Chicago Bar Constitutional Study Committee and the president of the Illinois League of Women Voters.[9] Three of these individuals had been members of the original Constitution Study Commission, although the commission as such was not involved in the campaign. (A second Constitution Study Commission was established in 1967 to prepare materials for the convention delegates; this commission proceeded on the assumption that the call would pass, although it did not become formally involved in the campaign for passage.) Throughout the summer of 1967, this informal committee solicited names of potential members on a statewide citizens' committee.[10] Letters of invitation to the weekly Wednesday luncheons were sent to representatives of organizations in the state that had expressed some positive concern for the upcoming constitutional referendum.

The Wednesday meetings culminated in a public meeting on October 25, 1967, at the Chicago Bar Association to which, in addition to those who had participated in the summer meetings, representatives of all significant civic, business, and professional groups in the state were invited. Approximately eighty people attended. The participants reflected the spirit of cooperation between civic and political adherents which in the past had been necessary for success in this type of constitutional venture. Yet doubts of a partisan nature prevailed. State Representative Paul Elward, Democrat from Chicago, attempted to alleviate fears concerning delegate makeup at the proposed convention—the same fears expressed earlier during legislative debate over the convention resolution. In

[8]Ibid., p. 81.

[9]Members of this initial planning committee were Samuel Witwer*, Elroy Sandquist, James Otis, Louis Ancel*, Jordan Hillman*, Peter Tomei, and Mary Helen Robertson. (Asterisks indicate those individuals who had been members of the Constitution Study Commission.)

[10]Taped interview with Peter Tomei, fall 1968.

response to an argument from the floor that the convention would reflect the same political bias as the Senate, Elward reasoned that the results in a number of senate districts that were primarily Republican had been so close that one or even two Democratic convention delegates could be elected from them.[11] As evidence will later indicate, it was a matter not so much of party as of "breed" of delegate that offset the potential for conservatism at the constitutional convention.

At this meeting, the Constitutional Committee Information Service (CCIS) was reinstated as an adjunct to the Illinois Committee for Constitutional Revision (ICCR), which served as an educational rather than a promotional organization and to which tax exempt contributions were filed. A steering committee of 13 was also elected; it included Elroy C. Sandquist, Jr., member of the convening committee, president of the City Club of Chicago, and chairman of the official opposition committee to the 1966 revenue amendment; Peter Tomei, chairman of the Chicago Bar Association Committee on Constitutional Revision; James T. Otis, attorney and member of the Constitution Study Commission; Robert Bergstrom, attorney, chairman of the special committee on the constitutional convention of the Union League Club of Chicago; Mrs. Elmer Carlson, legislative chairman of the Illinois Chapter, American Association of University Women; Timothy Murtaugh III, attorney, representing Illinois Jaycees; Wayne Stoneking, Executive Director of Illinois Education Association; Verna Larsen, president of Illinois Business and Professional Women's Clubs (she later dropped out because her organization did not endorse the proposed convention until late in the campaign); Charles Bane, attorney and editor of the *Chicago Bar Record*; Mary Helen Robertson, president of the Illinois League of Women Voters; Louis Ancel, attorney, member of the Constitution Study Commission, representing the Illinois Municipal League; Samuel W. Witwer, attorney and member of the Constitution Study Commission; and Peggy Norton, legislative chairmen of the Illinois Congress of Parents and Teachers. Legal, civic, and educational organizations dominated the committee membership. Missing at this early stage of campaign organization, although they later supported Con-Con, were the State Chamber of Commerce and the Illinois Agricultural Association. Labor opposition to the convention broke down later as well.

[11]Peter Tomei, Memorandum, Preliminary meeting for the organization of the 1967 statewide Citizens' Committee for Con-Con, October 30, 1968.

The major work of the enlarged steering committee was to approach the governor with a "pretested" list of possible chairmen for the state campaign committee. These carefully laid organizational plans were, in part, the result of lessons drawn from the aborted revenue campaign of 1966, when repeated attempts by the governor to appoint unwilling citizens as chairmen of the campaign committee got the revenue campaign off to a weak start. Hence, all individuals considered for this chairmanship would be screened for their willingness to serve in that capacity before the governor became publicly involved in the selection process.

Although names were offered and a list, subdivided into Chicago and downstate, was developed as early as the first meeting of the enlarged steering committee,[12] it was several weeks before members formally outlined their standards for selection of a chairman. Initially it was agreed that the cochairmen should consist of a business leader from Cook County and a farm leader from downstate (the original list had not included a downstate farm leader). Second, whether retired or not, the cochairmen should be sufficiently free from business and other commitments to devote virtually full time to the Con-Con effort. And third, one of the cochairmen might be a woman.[13] At a subsequent meeting, requirements for the Chicago-based chairman were adopted; he should be an outstanding civic leader not identified with the regular organization of either political party, and preference should be given to a prominent retired executive who could devote full time to the campaign or, if such a person could not be found, to an outstanding business executive who could devote a reasonable amount of time to heading the committee.[14]

A worked-over list of thirteen possible chairmen heavily favored business executives; six of the seven suggested for Chicago and three of the six for downstate were businessmen. No individuals representing a major organization in the state were on the list; this represented an attempt to break with the heavy organizational emphasis characteristic of most constitutional amendment campaigns in the past.

Delays in the governor's office at this point caused committee members to seek an alternative course. They agreed to appoint cochairmen without gubernatorial approval and thus avoid possible partisan fears induced by the governor's otherwise direct involve-

[12]Tomei, ICCR Steering Committee Memo, November 9, 1967.
[13]Tomei, ICCR Steering Committee Memo, December 6, 1967.
[14]Tomei, ICCR Steering Committee Memo, December 13, 1967.

ment in the selection process.[15] The committee decided to ask Joseph Block, retired chairman of Inland Steel, to chair the citizens' campaign committee. In the meantime, however, Witwer was able to schedule a meeting with Governor Kerner for late November to discuss the selection matter. Thereupon the steering committee shelved selection of the chairmen pending the results of that meeting.[16]

The appointments of Kingman Douglass, Jr., and William J. Kuhfuss, representing Chicago and downstate, respectively, were announced by the governor's office two months later. Neither had been on the list submitted by the citizens' committee, although Kuhfuss had been discussed in the meeting. Douglass, who had been suggested by Witwer after a search among his Commercial Club friends, proved an ideal choice. As an investment banker and member of the inner civic elite, he was in a position to assume the heavy financial role that a division of labor was later to place upon him. Kuhfuss, president of the Illinois Agricultural Association and the governor's choice, possessed the means, through local farm bureaus, to disseminate information downstate. Although neither man was well known, both fit the roles they would have to perform in the coming months.

The major responsibility of the steering committee had been facilitation of chairman selection; it is widely believed that the governor would not have acted in this capacity without prompting by such a group of citizens.[17] However, the committee had two other important functions: to obtain a tax-exempt status for campaign donations and to set up a headquarters from which the eventual chairmen and their workers could direct the campaign. Offices at 5 South Wabash were opened early in February under the temporary directorship of Peggy Norton with money left over from the accounts of the old ICCR.

The first formal meeting of the Illinois Committee for a Constitutional Convention (ICCC) was called by the newly appointed cochairmen on March 15, 1968. In attendance were Governor Kerner and a core group of members of the Board of Directors, invited by the governor. The steering committee assumed positions on the Board of Directors and handed their responsibility for campaign organization over to the permanent officers.

[15]Tomei, ICCR Steering Committee Memo, November 9, 1967.
[16]Tomei, ICCR Steering Committee Memo, November 29, 1967.
[17]Taped interview with William W. Allen, winter 1968.

The campaign for a constitutional convention was formally launched at the governor's luncheon in Springfield on April 17, 1968. Invited were some 100 business, labor, professional, agricultural, civic, and state political leaders. The object was promotional, and special attention was given to press and photographic releases. For example, participants, gathered according to geographic and interest groups, were photographed with the cochairmen and the governor and the pictures were sent to their local newspapers.

The luncheon theme, "Why My Group Favors Con Con," was carried out in speeches by representatives of legal, women's (LWV), labor (UAW only), educational (IEA), and agricultural (IAA) groups. Douglass and Kuhfuss, in a report on campaign and publicity plans, outlined what they believed would be the major campaign hurdles: "Our biggest campaign problems are voter apathy and the fact that we must compete for public attention in a presidential election year."[18]

PAPER BALLOT CONTROVERSY

Because obtaining approval for constitutional propositions in Illinois was so difficult, much attention had been focused from time to time on the form of ballot for such propositions. The danger of defeat at the polls in this popular election by numbers of apathetic voters prompted legislative reconsideration of this issue during special sessions in March and July. The Illinois Revised Statutes, 1965, Chapter 46, Sec. 16–6 contain a provision relating explicitly to constitutional amendments or to calling a constitutional convention. This is the blue ballot, approved by the Illinois General Assembly in 1949. The object of the blue color of the ballot was to attract the voters' attention and consequently reduce the traditionally high nonparticipation rate on constitutional questions. It was a technique that seemed to work in other states. Its first test in Illinois was the 1950 Gateway amendment, a proposal that sought to ease the requirement that constitutional amendments be approved by a majority of those voting in the general election; it allowed approval by two-thirds of those voting on the amendment itself. A significant number of constitutional amendments had earlier failed to secure approval because of the lack of voter participation on the question. To further ensure voter participation, the blue ballot bears two notices:

[18]ICCC press release, Chicago, April 12, 1968.

> The failure to vote this ballot is the equivalent of a negative vote. (This is not to be construed as a direction that your vote is required to be cast either in favor of or in opposition to the proposition herein contained.)
>
> Whether you vote this ballot or not you must return it to the Election Judge when you leave the voting booth.

Voters overwhelmingly approved the Gateway amendment at the 1950 general election, and the blue ballot has been used ever since for constitutional propositions.[19]

Despite the fact that the 1968 convention call would be presented on a blue ballot, fears persisted that it would be defeated. The threeway presidential race was stirring considerable interest nationwide, and a large November turnout was predicted. This meant that a significant number of persons who were usually nonvoters would show up at the polls. Such individuals would be expected to show little interest in any issue other than the presidential campaign, and the danger of voter nonparticipation on the constitutional proposition would thus be even greater than usual.

To get around this barrier, State Representative Harold Katz (Democrat, Glencoe) proposed the so-called party-circle ballot plan, in which the constitutional convention question would be placed on the regular ballot in such a way that the party position would be voted automatically by anyone casting a straight party vote, unless a vote against the party position was specifically indicated. Since both political parties in Illinois were expected to favor the convention, the automatic vote formula seemed to guarantee that the convention call would be approved. (Chicago Mayor Daley had not yet formally endorsed Con Con, but Democrats had wholeheartedly supported the convention resolution in a legislative session a year before.) The Katz plan received early support from the *Chicago Sun-Times:* "The Choice is between having the decision made by the apathy of the nonvoter or of assuming voter confidence in the party position unless otherwise indicated by the voter." [20]

Defense for the party-circle plan was based on historic precedent. Although State Senator Paul Simon, aspirant for lieutenant governor, publicly urged that the plan be rejected because "the straight party vote would be a radical departure from *our tradition* that issues must be voted on separately" (emphasis added),[21] nineteenth century ballots in Illinois indicate that party-circle voting was the

---

[19] Illinois Legislative Council, File 6–051–X, February 7, 1967.

[20] *Chicago Sun-Times*, February 20, 1968.

[21] *Peoria Journal*, May 11, 1968.

common practice then. In 1860, a ballot with a ticket headed by Abraham Lincoln for President carried the legend at the bottom of the party column, "For Convention." This referred to the call for the convention that met in 1862. It is apparent that votes on these party ballots would have been counted in favor of the convention unless this legend was scratched out.[22]

In the case of the 1868 election, which authorized the convention of 1869-70, several types of ballots can be found. On the Grant and Colfax (Republican) ballot used in Henry County, the legend read "FOR calling a convention to form a new constitution." Most Democratic ballots carried legends which read "AGAINST convention to form a new constitution." One "Democratic Ticket," identified as having been used in Warren County, offered the choice, "FOR . . . AGAINST . . . constitutional convention." On the former types, no action on the part of the voter was required to vote on the constitutional proposition, unless he disagreed with the position expressed on the ballot. In the latter case, the voter could scratch out the legends or change the "for" and "against" wording. It seems clear that the practice in 1860 and 1868 was for party organizations (usually at the county level) to take a position, if they desired, on constitutional propositions and express this position on the ballot.[23]

The change in the manner in which constitutional questions were submitted to popular vote was essentially circumstantial and occurred when Illinois revised its system of voting but did not change its constitution accordingly. The 1870 constitution provided that a majority of all persons voting in an election must approve any amendment to the basic charter or any call for a convention to rewrite it. Under the party ticket system, in which each party printed its own ballots, this was no real handicap. After the state began using the Australian ballot, in which the single ballot replaced separate party ballots, the voter specifically had to vote for or against an amendment; if he failed to do so, his ballot actually counted as a "no" vote. In 1892, the year after the adoption of the Australian ballot, the legislature put on the ballot a Gateway amendment to make the process of consitutional change conform to the new voting system. However, 80 percent of the voters simply did not bother to vote on it and the measure failed.[24] Bills of this nature were introduced in the legislative sessions of 1896, 1924, 1932, 1935,

[22]Illinois Legislative Council, File 6-761, May 13, 1968, p. 1.
[23]Ibid., p. 2.
[24]*Chicago Sun-Times*, March 31, 1968.

1937, 1938, 1939, 1941, 1943, and 1945. The irony was complete in 1946, when the governor explained his veto of a Gateway amendment, similar in intent to the 1892 proposal, as "an unusual, new, and tricky method of securing the approval of a constitutional amendment." He also noted that the attorney general was of the opinion that these measures were unconstitutional.[25]

Table I shows the relationship between the type of ballot and the rate of failure of constitutional propositions. Obviously, placing such a proposition on a separate ballot has an effect about halfway between the total success rates with party ballots and the total failure when propositions are placed on official nonpartisan ballots.

TABLE I. FAILURE RATE OF CONSTITUTIONAL PROPOSITIONS WITH VARIOUS TYPES OF BALLOTS

| Years | Ballot Presentation | Propositions | | Failure Rate (%) |
		No. Submitted	No. Approved	
1871 – 1890	Party ballot	5	5	0
1891 – 1898	Bottom of official ballot	3	0	100
1899 – 1929	Separate ballot	6	3	50
1930 – 1949	Side of official ballot	7	0	100
1950 – 1966[a]	Separate blue ballot	16	7	44

aSince 1950, the Gateway amendment has also been in effect; in fact, it was the first amendment passed with the blue ballot in 1950.

In 1968, opponents of the not-so-radical Katz proposal were of two types. One group opposed it because they opposed the entire idea of an unlimited constitutional convention and they believed the party-circle plan would enhance chances for success of the convention call in November. An attorney for the United Steelworkers argued,

> Although the Constitution clearly provides (Art. XIV, Sec. 1) that a constitutional convention can be called only if a majority voting at the election vote for a convention, these legislative leaders would apparently disregard this mandate by counting straight party votes for either party as votes for a constitutional convention. Their purpose is to achieve an artificial "majority" by flagrantly disregarding the actual intention of those straight-party voters who do not care to vote for Con-Con and who would not realize that they are in fact doing

[25]Illinois Legislative Council, File 6–090, February 6, 1967, p. 8.

so. . . . This arrogant scheme proves that its proponents will leave no stone unturned.[26]

Another group of party-circle opponents were actually strong and active supporters of the convention call. They believed, however, that a move on the part of the legislature to amend the statutes at this late date would indicate that proponents had serious doubts about passage of Con Con. "[If we] come along in the eleventh hour," explained Witwer,

> and change very basically the rules of the game . . . this would . . . afford a ready argument for opponents, and all we would succeed in doing would be to give the opposition a ready-made case for defeating [Con Con]. And I believe it would have been defeated. [In any case], I think [party circle balloting] is a rather dubious way to do constitutional amending. . . . I don't want to make it seem so darn easy that it becomes almost a decision of the political bosses of the two parties . . . to change the constitution.[27]

Witwer personally presented his arguments against the party-circle ballot to a number of newspapers, and the *Sun-Times* subsequently withdrew its editorial support of the Katz proposal. The effect of these maneuvers was to remove this ballot proposal from serious consideration by the legislature.[28]

An interesting historical note is the fact that, when Governor Stevenson proposed the party-circle formula for a convention call in 1949, support came from essentially nonpolitical groups such as the League of Women Voters and the Chicago Bar Association, while opposition came from labor, farm and manufacturing groups, the organizational bases of the political parties.

No sooner had this particular controversy been put to rest than a number of county officials demanded a change in the statutes so that they could place the constitutional question on the voting machines as separate items, rather than using blue ballots. Lake County officials claimed they could save the county $60,000 in election expenses.[29] Con Con proponents estimated a loss of hundreds of thousands of votes if this legislation passed. In fact, subsequent comparisons made on the participation rates for the constitutional question which remained on a separate blue ballot, and for other issues which had been placed on the machines, confirmed the predicted decline in awareness and hence, in the number of those

[26] *Chicago Sun-Times*, March 2, 1968.
[27] Taped interview with Samuel Witwer, fall 1968.
[28] Ibid.
[29] *Star*, Peoria, July 23, 1968.

voting on the machine entries. The average participation rate for these issues (a natural resources bond issue and a banking amendment) in the nine counties which used voting machines was approximately 30 percent less than the 87 percent participation rate for the Con Con question on a separate ballot.

Bills altering the ballot form and the voting regulations on constitutional questions were uniformly tabled in legislative committee. Despite these legislative decisions not to tamper with the election laws, the Cook County clerk, in the week before the election, placed the Con Con question on the machines within his jurisdiction—300,000 voting devices in approximately 3,000 precincts. Under threat of mandamus, however, the county official soon withdrew the Con Con question from the machines and again offered it to the voters, as in all other counties, on a separate blue sheet of paper. Once again it had been claimed that the county could save money and expedite counting by placing the question on the machines. Yet the action, however intended, was clearly illegal.[30] Considering the need for as much support as possible from this heavily populated, pro-amendment county, this incident was of major electoral significance.

[30] The attorney general ruled, August 1966, that election devices could not be used in the voting on constitutional amendments. Illinois Legislative Council, File 6–867, July 22, 1968.

III

The Campaign for Con Con Goes to the People

Vote "yes" on the Blue Ballot
Campaign slogan

A campaign may normally be divided into three distinct periods: organizational, educational, and promotional. In the campaign for a constitutional convention, the second or educational phase was, for all practical purposes, lacking. After almost a year of organizational activity the campaign, in the summer of 1968, moved directly into the promotional phase. The major reason for this was the decision by convention proponents to avoid antagonizing the opponents as much as possible. Thus low-level selling techniques were stressed, with unsubstantiated slogans and such general instructions as "Vote 'yes' on the Blue Ballot."

Development of the strategy began as early as October 1967, before the formal campaign organization jelled. Members of the initial steering committee felt that a successful campaign had to elicit: (1) strong support from both political parties; (2) unremitting support from the mass media; and (3) support from civic, business, professional, agricultural, and labor organizations—in short, total support from those groups capable of mobilizing significant numbers of voters. Such support, by definition, required an issueless format, for beyond the basic agreement to call a convention lay broad ideological and practical differences.

In order to secure this wide support, it was considered necessary to have—in addition to the statewide citizens' committee which would provide centralized leadership—a finance committee, local campaign committees, a campaign theme, adequate literature, and a campaign timetable.[1]

FINANCE COMMITTEE

In Chicago, about $250 million a year is raised by public subscription for charitable purposes. Fund raisers are of two general types: persons of great wealth who contribute money generously and representatives of the large corporations that put up most of the money in practically all drives. According to one of the cochairmen of the campaign committee:

> In the city of Chicago there is a group called the Commercial Club. The Commercial Club is a composium of the prominent businessmen of the area, about 250 to 300 men. The Commercial Club represents . . . the leadership of most of the activities of a civic nature that occur in the city. . . . Whenever such need arose . . . people turned historically to the Commercial Club.[2]

The drive for a constitutional convention was no exception, and once again leadership was sought from the ranks of the Commercial Club. Kingman Douglass had no particular experience in public campaigning as such, but he was in a position to solicit the funds required to conduct a convention call campaign. As in all constitutional amendment campaigns, no public monies had been appropriated for this purpose.

Douglass prevailed upon a number of Commercial Club members to form the nucleus of a finance committee. This organization was not part of the regular citizens' campaign committee and assumed no responsibility beyond its fund-raising role. In five months, the finance committee raised over $235,000 of which $210,000 had come from heads of business. Only a few major contributions, such as John Deere and Caterpillar Tractor, were not Chicago based. Generally, appeals were directed to known contributors to most civic causes. The subject of the cause appeared irrelevant. One of the two principal sources for potential donors was the Chicago Symphony list. The approach was always personal.

> It is sort of a fraternal thing . . . and I call and say, Joe, remember last year when you were chairman of the ABC campaign? I gave you $3,000. I'm going to need a little more than that this time. I need a check for $5,000. . . . It's a club. . . . Without [these contacts] you

[1]Pre-campaign Outline for the Blue Ballot Constitutional Convention Referendum, October 25, 1967, CCIS (mimeo).
[2]Taped interview with Kingman Douglass, October 25, 1968.

are not in. We didn't have them last time in revenue [revenue amendment campaign of 1966]. The guy who was trying to raise our money was not a member of the fraternity.[3]

The majority of contributing businesses donated $8,000, the maximum amount requested by the committee.[4] Most contributors did not demand tax deductibility. For those who did, however, a separate committee was incorporated to receive tax-deductible contributions. Approximately $90,000 was made available to the Constitutional Convention Information Service (CCIS), which according to federal regulation had to be spent on educational and informational programs, and not promotional items. In other words, tax-deductible money could be spent on materials requesting people to vote in the referendum, but not to urge them to vote "yes" on the question. The balance of roughly $135,000 was bound over to the ICCC without stipulation as to use.

Few attempts were made to solicit donations from individuals at the $5 and $10 levels, since it was felt that the returns would not justify the time and effort required for such a project. Nevertheless, contact for smaller contributions was made through three existing channels. Adlai Stevenson III, a known sympathizer of constitutional reform, was asked to add an item for Con Con contributions in one of his newsletters to supporters. The letter had a distribution of about 16,000. The ICCC picked up the $800 cost of the letter, hoping only to recover the initial financial outlay and gain 16,000 constitutional convention voters. As a result of the letter, however, the ICCC received $3,000 worth of individual contributions.

Similarly, Otto Kerner, the former Democratic governor, was asked to write to a number of his friends. About $3,500 was added to ICCC finances as a result of about eighty personal letters. Lastly, the Chicago Bar Association distributed letters signed by twelve prominent lawyers among its members; this effort earned an additional $2,000.

No organizations contributed to the ICCC fund, with the exceptions of $5,000 contributions from the Republican and Democratic parties. Endorsing groups expended their resources internally in an attempt to educate their own memberships. In addition, local citizens' committees throughout at least two-thirds of the state were encouraged to raise their own campaign funds.

The projected campaign budget of over $300,000 was not reached. The first area to suffer was the media campaign. To com-

[3]Taped interview with William Allen, winter 1968.
[4]Taped interview with Kingman Douglass, October 25, 1968.

plicate the tight money situation, strategists had underestimated the demand for materials, which increased dramatically after the 1968 national conventions. ICCC officers were split on the matter of real-locating funds to compensate for this demand. Each penny shifted to the materials outlay cut into the already diminished fund for publicity. If the convention call referendum had failed, major blame would undoubtedly have been placed upon the media squeeze in the last weeks of the campaign.

LOCAL CITIZENS' COMMITTEES

Since it was feared that it would stretch resources too far, citizen groups were organized in the cities of only 22 counties; the areas not covered tended to be in the southeastern part of the state. These committees were to serve two basic purposes: to demonstrate evidence of a groundswell within the state for constitutional revision, and to motivate grassroots support for the convention referendum. Neither objective was entirely realized. In the first place, there was no groundswell for constitutional reform; rather, major state organizations with local affiliates, specifically the League of Women Voters[5] and the Illinois Congress of Parents and Teachers, were instrumental in establishing at least some core groups.[6] Secondly, the state president of the League of Women Voters seriously doubted the ability of her association to form groups at the local level which would involve the entire community.[7] Hence, so-called grassroots support was primarily organizational. The groups represented were overwhelmingly business, civic, or professional.[8] Nevertheless, the local committees served as useful propaganda tools: "down home" activity almost invariably carries the indelible impression of "by the people."[9]

The importance of the downstate committees as purveyors of information about the constitutional convention was somewhat dissipated by the decision of ICCC officers not to open downstate offices as had been common in previous amendment campaigns. "We wished to avoid diversionary tactics," explained cochairman

[5]This is common practice for Leagues in other states as well. *Inventory Revision by State League of Women Voters* (Washington: The League of Women Voters, December 1960).

[6]Taped interview with Mary Helen Robertson, fall 1968.

[7]Taped interview with Mary Helen Robertson, fall 1968.

[8]ICCC, Organization Kit for Local Con Con Committees, (undated), p. 2.

[9]Roscoe Martin, *Grass Roots* (University of Alabama Press: Birmingham, 1957), p. 5.

Douglass.[10] However, stress upon Chicago-based operations not only weakened the status and role of downstate committees but undoubtedly hindered formation of other citizens' groups. The natural hostility to Chicago "operations" shared by most downstate dwellers must not be underrated.

The ICCC spent somewhat more than $20,000 on local citizens' committees and hired field workers to help set them up. However, the great majority of committees had already been formed by June 1968, when the downstate field workers undertook their duties. Most of the committees were designed to cover a senatorial district, a county, a suburban division, a city division (in Chicago), a cluster of cities such as the Quad Cities, or a single city. Many county committees were, in effect, merely city commitees. The functions of these local campaign committees varied only by degree. Most established speakers bureaus, distributed materials, purchased newspaper advertising, sponsored an activity such as a parade or a booth at a county fair, and generally sought sympathetic editorial support for the convention referendum.

CAMPAIGN THEMES

One of the "firsts" in the campaign for a constitutional convention was the employment of a survey research organization. Its role was to supply the ICCC and its advertising agency with in-depth information on the awareness, perception, and ballot strength of the call for a constitutional convention and to test potential campaign themes and slogans.[11]

In particular, the survey findings demonstrated the potential for circular reinforcement of specific cues or campaign themes. Those who claimed normally to vote for an issue on the blue ballot were asked to cite their reasons. Respondents suggested that, on the whole, the blue ballot represents improvement and reform.

By way of contrast, those who normally vote "no" on blue ballot issues do so principally because they believe constitutional revision raises taxes. Initially, then, campaign strategists knew that the blue ballot, regardless of issue, had a positive significance for many voters and that tax issues should be avoided whenever possible. This latter proviso was difficult to follow since major convention opponents argued that the constitutional convention was a complicated

---

[10]Taped interview, fall 1968.

[11]Market Opinion Research, *1968 Illinois Pre-Election Study* (Chicago, Illinois, August 1968). Sample Size: 800

Electing a Constitution

TABLE I. REASONS FOR FAVORABLE VOTE ON BLUE BALLOT ISSUES
(Summer 1968)

Blue ballot issues are for the better	22.9%
Need improvement	22.9
Civic improvement	16.7
Depends on issue	16.0
Recommended by group	7.6
Better education	5.6
Other	8.3
(N = 800)	100.0

attempt to rewrite the revenue articles; this was a touchy point since precisely such an attempt had been made and failed two years earlier.

In a nondirective survey question (i.e., one that has no predetermined list from which to select responses) voters who had said they were for the convention call gave a variety of reasons for their feelings. As Table II indicates, the majority of respondents believed the constitution needed updating or changing. Another survey conducted at about the same time also found that people felt the constitution needed updating (83 percent).[12] However, respondents in the same survey strongly disagreed with the statement that the 1870 constitution was "one of the worst." While many felt, therefore, that the constitution should be brought into line with contemporary needs, few were willing to condemn the document as totally useless or irrelevant.

TABLE II. REASONS FOR FAVORING A CONVENTION CALL
(Summer 1968)

	Total
Needs updating/changes	66.7%
For good of the people	10.6
Fair tax system	4.9
Solve problems/improve conditions	3.7
Increase awareness	3.3
Strengthen laws	2.0
Other	1.6
No reason	10.2
(N = 800)	103.0

[12]University of Illinois, *Omnibus Study: The Constitutional Convention Referendum* (Urbana, Illinois, September 1968). Sample Size: 3000

It is not surprising that the overriding campaign theme for the constitutional convention focused on the notion of updating the 100-year-old Illinois constitution. The image of the horse-and-buggy era transposed upon a jet-age scene was popular. The most common parade entry at county fairs was, predictably, the horse and buggy (an old horse and a battered buggy). The theme was simple, catchy, and effective as a recruiting and reinforcing device.

The survey also showed that with just a few short months to go only 25 percent of the population had heard about the constitutional convention. In both the Chicago area and downstate 66 percent of the people had "not heard or seen anything about con-con" and 9 percent did not know whether or not they had heard about it. The problem for the campaign strategists was how to reach a sufficient number of people who would go to the polls.

It is interesting to note that the belief that awareness of political questions and voter activity are related was reaffirmed by these surveys on the convention call. As the following table shows, the most active voters were also the most aware voters on the Con Con issue.

TABLE III. VOTER HISTORY AND AWARENESS OF CON CON
(Summer 1968)

Voting Activity	Aware of Con Con*
Always vote	36%
Vote very often	35
Vote sometimes	22
Hardly ever or never vote	17
	110

*Figures are those provided by the survey.

Survey respondents were asked how they intended to vote on the convention call. A few opposed a constitutional convention, but most were undecided.

A majority of the undecided voters were so because they possessed little or no information about the constitutional convention. At that time a report by the public relations firm of the ICCC claimed that 75 percent of voters would vote "yes" on the constitutional question if they were made aware of the issue. Hence, the ICCC in the months ahead had to create massive voter awareness if the convention question was to receive a positive majority of the 65-70 percent voter turnout expected in the 1968 presidential election.

TABLE IV. CON CON VOTE INTENTIONS
(Summer 1968)

	Total	Rep.*	Ticket Splitters*	Dem.*
Yes	30.8%	34.2%	35.9%	26.8%
No	4.4	4.4	8.0	3.4
Not voting	4.3	3.7	1.9	5.1
Don't know/undecided	60.5	54.0	58.7	63.8
(N = 800)	100.0	96.3	104.5	99.1

*Figures are those provided by the survey.

TABLE V. REASONS FOR UNDECIDED VOTE
(Summer 1968)

	Total
Haven't heard about it	35.0%
Don't understand it	28.0
Inadequate information	17.8
May not go to the polls and vote	1.2
Depends on proposed changes	1.0
Don't know	17.0
(N = 800)	100.0

A survey in September confirmed the public relations report. A strong majority (62 percent) said they would vote "yes," only 10 percent said they would vote "no," and somewhat over a quarter (27.3 percent) were undecided; 0.7 percent gave no answer. If the two studies were correct, the percentage of "yes" voters had doubled, while the proportion of undecided voters halved. As undecided voters became aware of Con Con, they were indeed moving more often into the "yes" ranks than into the negative ranks. This is contrary to the findings in a number of referendum election studies which show a relationship between low turnouts and success and greater turnouts and electoral defeat. It appears, therefore, that voting behavior may depend on the type of information conveyed. The Con Con campaign strategists had a simple message to put over. More sophisticated concepts were not only unnecessary at this juncture of constitutional revision but potentially devastating. In fact, so superficial had been many voters' contact with the Con Con issue that only six months after the election a majority of respondents to a poll did not remember hearing anything about altering the constitution or about the election to call a convention.[13]

The upshot of all this was that the ICCC made extensive use of the simple slogan "Vote 'Yes' on the Blue Ballot." It was felt that this would be effective because evidence indicated that (a) some voters were already inclined to relate the blue ballot and "good government," and (b) other voters made aware of the issue—even a simple instruction to vote on the question—would overwhelmingly vote affirmatively.

Awareness of the issue, however, had little to do with understanding it. For example, respondents to the postelection survey were asked to read three related themes on a card and then asked if they had been aware of, understood, and believed the theme. The three themes, based essentially on the simple vote concept, were: theme A, "Vote for the Blue Ballot November 5, Vote for Illinois;" theme B, "Vote for the Blue Ballot November 5, Vote for yourself;" and theme C, "Vote 'Yes' on the Blue Ballot." The highest awareness, understanding, and believability levels among voters were for theme "C." Even a majority of those who voted against the convention call were aware of this theme, although fewer claimed they understood it. Of those who did not vote on the issue, more had not heard of the theme (39 percent) then had (32 percent). The remainder could not remember. What is interesting here is not that a voter is aware of a specific campaign theme, but what he means when he claims to understand a slogan and believe its message. The simple instruction of theme "C" is clearly understandable. But what does the statement contain that requires belief? The answer lies in the history of the blue ballot itself: blue ballot propositions automatically trigger notions of "better government" in the minds of many voters. Not surprisingly, believability levels among "no" voters were low (25.5 percent). Themes "A" and "B" were less familiar and less understood.

Concrete issues were not generally a part of the campaign for a constitutional convention. It was hoped that the simple impetus to vote would be sufficient to carry the question. The opinion surveys, however, attempted to probe voters' motivation. Respondents were asked to list the most important problems facing Illinois. The two most frequently cited issues were race and high taxes. But when asked if the constitutional convention would solve the race problem,

[13]Market Opinion Research, *1968 Illinois After Election Study* (Chicago, Illinois, January 1969). Sample Size: 800

respondents more often said "no" than "yes." Many also claimed that a new constitution would mean higher taxes in the form of a state income tax. Yet, many of these same respondents supported the convention call. Negative voters believed things were in much poorer shape than did the others and obviously did not see a constitutional convention as a means of correcting these deficiencies. In other words, voters did not appear to connect basic problems with a need to revise the constitution. This superficiality was, of course, not disturbed by the type of campaign being waged for approval of the Illinois Con Con.

CAMPAIGN LITERATURE

Altogether the ICCC distributed over ten million brochures, fliers, bumper stickers, buttons, and 2.5 million sample ballots. Channels for distribution were primarily the local citizens' committees, and, secondarily, endorsing organizations. An insignificant amount of material was distributed to individuals on a personal basis. The major portion of materials, including two million sample ballots, was given out in the Chicago metropolitan area by political organizations.

Endorsing organizations similarly distributed Con Con information and promotional materials for their members, usually through their normal communications channels (e.g. newsletters). Roughly four million people were reached by these organizational means.[14] Generally, material distributed by endorsees attempted to answer two questions: (a) does the Illinois Constitution *need* revision? and (b) is the constitutional convention the *best method* for changing the constitution? With the notable exceptions of the Chicago Bar Association and League of Women Voters, none of the groups tried to give substantive responses to these questions. To the first query, the common response was, "Yes, Illinois state government must be modernized;" to the second, a popular answer was, "Yes, because the piecemeal or amendment approach to constitutional revision is practically impossible."

Despite the considerable quantity of materials about the constitutional convention, the principal source for voter information was the news media. In the survey conducted during the summer prior to the election, respondents who had heard or seen anything about

---

[14]Taped interview with William Allen, winter 1968.

the convention call (roughly one-third) cited the following sources for their information (only first choices were recorded): newspapers, 33 percent; television, 30.9 percent; politicians, 9 percent; radio, 6 percent; literature, letters, brochures, 3 percent; magazines, 2 percent; League of Women Voters, 2 percent; and 14.4 percent did not know. A postelection survey reaffirmed these findings on the importance of the news media as sources of voter information.[15] In response to the question, "From where did you receive your information about Con Con?" (with more than one choice being permitted), 75.1 percent said newspapers; 54.6 percent mentioned television; and 21.1 percent mentioned radio.

Little media time or space was purchased by opponents to the constitutional convention. Opposition literature was distributed by both formal organizations, principally the AFL-CIO, as well as ad hoc associations such as the Committee to Oppose a Con Con in Illinois, headquartered in Quincy, and a Save our State Committee (SOS) of Winnetka (formerly the Save our Suburbs and Save our Schools committees). There was no apparent coordination of activity among the groups. In fact, the reasons presented by groups opposing the convention call frequently contradicted one another. On the one hand, labor stressed a "soak the poor" theme which warned that the convention would be controlled by business interests, especially with regard to rewriting revenue provisions. On the other hand, the ad hoc groups, which represented essentially right-wing beliefs, warned of impending socialism in the form of constitutional restrictions upon private property, neighborhood schools, and freedom of choice.[16]

Some opposed the convention because they believed that "Dreamers and do-gooders are behind the Con-Con. . . . Those who will serve on the convention will not be the objective people because these people will be unable to spend long periods of time from their jobs to do this work."[17]

All opponents attempted to counter the arguments that the constitution was old and needed revision. They argued, for example, that the 1870 Illinois constitution was one hundred years *younger* than the United States Constitution,[18] and that a constitution was a sacred document not to be tampered with. Thus, state AFL–CIO President Ruben Soderstrom claimed: "There are some things you

[15] *1968 Illinois After Election Study.*

[16] *Save Our State*, Winnetka, undated brochure.

[17] Troy Kost of the Township Officials of Illinois in *Telegraph*, Alton, April 30, 1968.

[18] Illinois Committee for Home Rule, Breese, undated pamphlet.

don't change—the Lord's Prayer, the Sermon on the Mount, the Ten Commandments and the Illinois Constitution."[19]

Convention proponents were seriously concerned about the possible effects of the negative campaign waged by the AFL–CIO among its one million members. It too had a simple slogan, "Don't be Conned into Con Con," and used an estimated $50,000 in its efforts.[20] However, labor was split, with the United Auto Workers and a handful of smaller unions endorsing the constitutional convention. As it turned out, union leaders ultimately had little effect on how their members voted on the blue ballot. Sixty-two percent of AFL–CIO members, responding to the postelection survey, claimed to have supported the convention call, while only 50 percent of UAW members said they had voted affirmatively.

FINAL PHASE OF THE CAMPAIGN

The campaign, measured in terms of the demand for materials, films and speakers, picked up dramatically after Labor Day. In this last phase, an attempt was made to secure support among the great number of people who did not belong to organizations. Promotion in the "action months" of September and October was characterized by an increased use of the media and distribution of materials in a nonstructured way such as through street handouts.

In response to advice from earlier research, the ICCC began extensive advertising in the print media approximately four weeks before the election; radio advertising began two weeks later; and use of television was concentrated almost entirely in the last few days. Television advertising was limited by available resources and was beamed primarily to major metropolitan areas throughout the state, with the exception of East St. Louis. Approximately twice as many ten-second spots were purchased in Chicago as anywhere else. The ICCC did not avail itself of public service time, which would have given the opposition an opportunity to secure equal time—a lesson which may have been learned from the abortive Maryland constitutional campaign.

Nonstructured dissemination of information also increased. This included distribution of roughly 3.5 million grocery shopping bags marked "Vote Yes on the Blue Ballot" through outlets of a major grocery chain in Illinois a week prior to the election,[21] and 1.8 mil-

---

[19] *Rockford Register-Republic*, May 4, 1968.
[20] *Chicago Tribune*, September 25, 1968.
[21] ICCC News Release, August 20, 1968.

lion blue ballot reminders to be taken home by Illinois school children the day before the election. The reminders were not intended to tell parents how to vote but merely to make them aware of the issue and to urge them to go to the polls. Earlier research had demonstrated the positive effects of nondirective "vote" instructions.

Blue Ballot Week was declared by Governor Shapiro in mid-October. The principal function of the week was a Chicago Bar Association dinner in Chicago. Ward and township committeemen of both parties were invited to it in an attempt to solicit their active support on the constitutional issue. Both gubernatorial candidates were present, as were the leaders of the largest party conferences, Republican Edmund Kucharski and Democrat Richard J. Daley. Only 55 of 160 invited party workers and a handful of representatives from endorsing organizations attended. In all, 200 people came.

There was no question that the parties' primary efforts were focused on the election of candidates to national and state office. However, precinct workers did distribute over two million sample blue ballots in Cook County. Another quarter million were distributed by county parties downstate.

A final and crucial function of the ICCC was a personal letter to all county clerks in the state reminding them of blue ballot voting procedures. It pointed out that in those counties using voting machines, according to Section 17–9 of the Election Code, individuals must vote the blue ballot first and deposit it in the ballot box before being permitted to enter the voting booth; furthermore, in all counties the blue ballots must be placed on top of all other paper ballots as they are handed to the voters.

Some ICCC spokesmen believed that the campaign had peaked early, and the final task of the organization was to sustain interest among the voters. However, the postelection survey indicated that roughly 40 percent of the respondents did not decide they would vote on the issue until the last two weeks of the campaign (had they not voted on the question, of course, these would have been treated as "no" votes). These were voters who had received their information about Con Con in the final days when the campaign assumed a heavy media emphasis. They represented nonstructured groups whose communications channels had been only marginally infiltrated by earlier Con Con information, since such information had flowed principally through the network of state and local organizations. Hence, the accelerated timetable and increased expenses during the so-called action months were necessary ingredients of the successful campaign.

IV

Con Con Election Analysis

It was a unique election year.

Hubert Humphrey

Illinois voters approved the convention call by nearly a three-to-one margin: 2.9 million voted "yes" on the ballot, while the "no" votes totalled 1.1 million. As indicated in the table below,[1] more Democrats than Republicans voted in the election and also voted "yes" on the convention call. Even more interesting, however, is the fact that more Democrats than Republicans also chose not to vote at all on the convention call issue. In fact, it is the nonparticipant that is most interesting in this election. In addition, any analysis of the Con Con election must also take into account the peculiar situation at the national level during the 1968 presidential campaign.

TABLE I. PARTY PREFERENCE AND BLUE BALLOT PARTICIPATION

Total Voting in Election		Voting on Convention Call		
		Yes	No	Didn't Vote
Democrats	37.7%	37.6%	33.6%	40.3%
Ticket Splitters	29.4	31.9	32.0	21.5
Republicans	31.1	29.9	32.0	32.9
Not Stated	2.0	.6	2.4	5.3
(N = 800)	100.2	100.0	100.0	100.0

[1]Market Opinion Research, *1968 Illinois After Election Study* (Chicago, Illinois, January 1969). Sample Size: 800

NONPARTICIPANTS, WALLACE, AND ALIENATION

The year 1968 was an interesting one for national politics. A third presidential party actually threatened the primacy of the American two-party system by creating the very real possibility that the president could be chosen by the House of Representatives. The American Independent party of presidential aspirant George Wallace did not have the votes (in terms of either a national plurality or an electoral college majority) to assure a political victory, but Wallace was creating for himself a potential bargaining position within a system of government programed by compromise. Ultimately, Wallace did deny both Richard Nixon and Hubert Humphrey an absolute majority by polling approximately ten million votes (forty-six electoral college votes) for 13.5 percent of the presidential vote.

Con Con proponents had feared that this Wallace-type conservatism would undermine the attempt at constitutional revision in Illinois.[2] The fear turned out to be unfounded. Not only did the American Independent party win only 8.5 percent of the state's vote,[3] conservative sentiments did not affect the state at all. In fact, presidential voting patterns returned to the geographic patterns that had existed prior to 1964, the year in which the Johnson-Goldwater election had had such a disturbing effect on traditional voting patterns in Illinois as well as other states.[4]

Another major fear of constitutional convention proponents—that the number of nonparticipants on the Con Con question would be high enough to defeat the measure—also did not materialize. In fact, the overall participation rate (the percentage of voters in the election who voted on the convention question) was the highest recorded for a constitutional proposal since Gateway had passed in 1950. Furthermore, as indicated in Figure 1, the average rate of nonparticipation in counties approving the call was only 12.4 percent, while in counties not approving the convention call the nonparticipation rate averaged 24 percent. Despite the high overall participation rate, nonvoting contributed to defeat in nine counties.

The relationship between voting for Wallace and voting on the convention call was interesting. Although "no" votes for Con Con and support for Wallace were not comparable statistically, the Wal-

[2]Taped interview with Kingman Douglass, October 25, 1968.
[3]Richard Scammon, *America Votes—8: A Handbook of Contemporary American Election Statistics* (Washington, D.C.: Governmental Affairs Institute, 1979).
[4]Everett G. Smith, Jr. "Twentieth Century Voting Patterns for President in Illinois," *Illinois Government* 32, (January 1970), p. 7.

TABLE II. VOTE ON THE CALL FOR A CONVENTION
(by area of the state)

Area	No. of Proposals Approved since 1952	% Voting "Yes"* of those Voting in Election	% Voting "Yes" of those Voting on Call
Cook County	11	71.4	80.3
Chicago City	11	68.7	81.2
Suburban	11	75.5	79.1
Downstate	1	55.1	64.1
Statewide	6	63.3	72.4

*Constitutional majority.

lace vote and the nonparticipation rate on the constitutional question did evidence a pattern. In forty-six counties the nonparticipation rate was below 15 percent and only four of these counties accorded Wallace over 10 percent of their presidential vote. However, of the fifty-six counties in which the nonparticipation rate exceeded 15 percent, 24 counties—or 43 percent—gave Wallace over 10 percent of their vote. These figures may represent the degree of political alienation. Popularly defined in terms of reaction to the prevailing system, political alienation may be expressed either through negative voting or through failure to vote. Political analysts have attributed much of the Wallace vote in 1968 to a negative response by many Americans to the political environment as they perceived it at that time. A vote for Wallace was, in fact, a vote against the "established" two-party system. But the Wallace vote and the blue ballot nonvote are not consistent modes of behavior although their root may be political alienation. In other words, some people reflect alienated feelings by opting out of the election game altogether—the "stay-at-homes"—while others of the same persuasion manifest themselves in negative voting behavior. One can only assume that, while not altogether mutually exclusive, the politically alienated normally pursue one or the other course of action, not both simultaneously. It is, therefore, highly unlikely that the Wallace vote and nonparticipation are related on this particular issue by the bond of alienation.

NONPARTICIPANTS AND PARTICIPANTS: WHO WERE THEY?

The 1968 blue ballot election provides researchers with another opportunity to speculate about why some people vote and others do not. A tendency profile of the nonparticipant in this election shows him to have had little formal education, a low income (less than $6,000), to be older, a black, and a home renter. This was in sharp contrast to the typical "yes" voter who had a high school or even postgraduate education, had a middle to upper-level income, was relatively young, and white. The "no" voter does not show such a pattern: he was likely to come from any educational or income level.

TABLE III. EDUCATION AND VOTE ON CONSTITUTIONAL REFERENDUM

	Yes	No	Did not Vote on Con Con
Total	59.8%	16.4%	23.8%
Grade school & less	46.9	14.8	38.3
Some high school	49.0	17.0	34.0
Graduated high school	65.6	18.5	15.8
Some college	65.7	15.7	18.7
College graduate	78.6	10.7	10.7
Post graduate	75.0	16.7	8.3
Refused to answer	16.7	16.7	66.7

TABLE IV. INCOME AND VOTE ON CONSTITUTIONAL REFERENDUM

	Yes	No	Did not Vote on Con Con
Total	59.8%	16.4%	23.8%
$ 0–2,299	33.8	21.6	44.6
$3,00–4,999	47.7	12.5	39.8
$5,000–5,999	45.8	16.9	37.3
$6,000–6,999	56.9	13.8	29.3
$7,000–9,999	76.0	13.7	10.3
$10,000–14,999	65.0	19.4	15.6
$15,000–24,999	76.1	14.9	9.0
$25,000 and over	73.9	17.4	8.7
Refused to answer	50.8	16.7	32.5

N = 800

The election also appears to show that voters who usually voted "no" on constitutional questions did not alter their behavior for the 1968 blue ballot. In the postelection survey, only 1.5 percent of those who said they had voted in favor of Con Con claimed that they "normally" voted "no" on blue ballot questions. Yet, eighteen of the fifty-seven counties which had seldom, if ever, supported constitutional issues in the past did approve the 1968 call. It seems likely, then, that these "yes" votes were pulled from the ranks of those who were usually nonparticipants and from among new voters. Unless large numbers of "no" voters stayed at home in 1968, the number of participants in these normally "negative" counties must have increased for this election. In fact, there was a 7 percent increase in voter turnout throughout the state.

WHERE AND WHY CON CON WON

Numerous factors contributed to the blue ballot success of 1968. Ultimately the most important of these may well have been the historical inclination of certain counties to support constitutional reform and the fact that most of these counties represent the major population centers in the state. These were also the areas in which the primary communication efforts were made. The statewide Citizens' Committee for a Constitutional Convention, headquartered in Chicago, followed a strategy calling for the greatest exposure for the least cost and effort. This obviously called for a heavy emphasis on condensed population centers for radio, TV, and newspaper coverage. Despite this strategy, the historical perspective was no doubt of great significance.

Using Thomas Kitsos' categories for showing support for constitutional amendments during the previous twenty years,[5] and comparing that record with the 1968 blue ballot results, we find that,

> on balance, counties which had "strongly negative" voting records on the past fifteen amendments tended to reject the call for the convention. Of the 57 counties identified as "strongly negative," 39 failed to return a constitutional majority. Also, in 19 counties, a majority of those voting on the issue voted "no." Sixteen of these 19 counties were labeled "strongly negative."[6]

Table V shows how the counties, using the Kitsos categories, voted on Con Con.

[5] Thomas R. Kitsos, "Constitutional Amendments and the Voter, 1952–1966," Commission Papers of the Institute of Government and Public Affairs, University of Illinois (Urbana, 1968), p. 10.

[6] Thomas Kitsos, "Constitutional Amendments and the Call for the Sixth Illinois Constitutional Convention" (Addendum to "Constitutional Amendments and the Voter, 1952–1966"), mimeographed (undated).

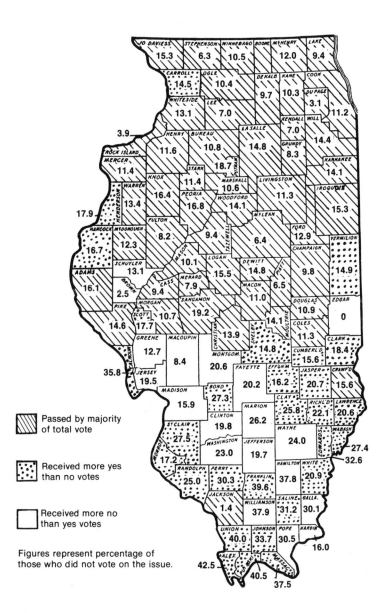

FIGURE I. VOTING ON CONVENTION CALL

Passed by majority
of total vote

Received more yes
than no votes

Received more no
than yes votes

Figures represent percentage of
those who did not vote on the issue.

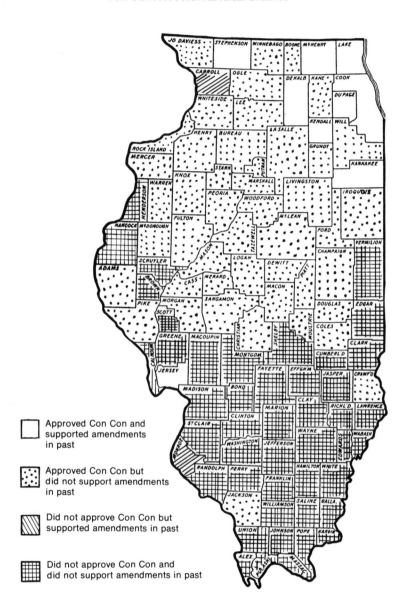

FIGURE II. VOTE ON CON CON AND HISTORY OF SUPPORT
FOR CONSTITUTIONAL AMENDMENTS

☐ Approved Con Con and
supported amendments
in past

▨ Approved Con Con but
did not support amendments
in past

▧ Did not approve Con Con but
supported amendments in past

▦ Did not approve Con Con and
did not support amendments in past

TABLE V. CON CON VOTE BY COUNTY TYPE

County Type	Yes	No	Total	Approval
Strong support	8	2	10	80%
Mildly negative	28	7	35	80%
Strongly negative	18	39	57	30%
Total	54	48	102	53%

The forty-eight counties that voted "no" are located almost entirely in the southern half of the state. Figure 2 indicates which counties failed to give a constitutional majority to the Con Con proposition, which maintained a tradition by doing so, and which broke with tradition by doing so. It is clear where anticonvention sentiments were strongest. It is equally clear that county voting patterns since 1952 are related to the 1968 vote on the convention proposition.

Although most counties with strongly negative histories voted against Con Con, the exceptions were notable: for example, Knox, Woodford, Iroquois, Sangamon, Crawford, Christian, Moultrie, and Douglas counties, which had approved only one of the fifteen previous amendments, all supported the calling of the convention. Perhaps the most noteworthy example was Coles County. This east central Illinois county had not given a constitutional majority to any proposed amendment since Gateway. Yet, 50.1 percent of those who voted in Coles County at the 1968 general election voted "yes" for the convention. Those who claim that citizens' committees played an indispensable role in passing Con Con might take comfort in the fact that in approximately half of these counties which defied their traditional position on constitutional matters in 1968, local Con Con groups were at work. It should also be noted, however, that Carroll and Monroe counties, which had been strong supporters of constitutional reform previously, did not approve the convention call, although in both counties more "yes" than "no" votes were cast. Both had relatively high participation rates on the question. The average nonparticipation rate for counties lacking the constitutional majority but voting "yes" more often than "no" on the question was 25 percent. Yet, the rates for Carroll and Monroe counties were 14.5 percent and 13.7 percent respectively.

It is significant that twenty-eight of the thirty-five counties typed as "mildly negative" toward constitutional reform approved the convention call. Yet, the collective plurality for these twenty-eight counties totalled 98,416 votes; when compared to the half million Cook County plurality, these results take on different proportions. Adding together the pluralities for the eight counties classed as traditionally "supportive" of constitutional reform, it appears that passage of the blue ballot question by any other counties in 1968 was only icing on the cake. However, from the perspective of a nascent constitutional consensus, the broader-based geographic distribution of support is significant. The Illinois Constitution belongs to all the people of the state and not solely to the voters of the Chicago metropolitan area.

ELECTION RETURNS AND ELECTION METHODS

Although isolated factors cannot conclusively explain voting patterns, the role of voting machines was crucial to electoral behavior in the 1968 blue ballot election. Nine counties, representing the major metropolitan areas of the state, utilized voting machines in their polling places. On the machine, along with all lists of candidates for national, state, and local office, were two separate questions—a proposed amendment to the Banking Act and a Natural Resources bond issue. Constitutional questions, however, cannot be placed on the electronic devices but must be handed out separately as blue paper ballots to each voter at the polls. Comparative returns on these issues indicate widely divergent participation rates which must, in large measure, be attributed to the voting mechanism.

Comparison of the participation rates for the bond issue and for the banking amendment in "electronic" counties and paper ballot counties demonstrates the fact that voters are more likely to disregard issues on a voting machine—whose ballot naturally emphasizes candidates for office—than they are when paper ballots are used for all electoral items.[7] In three-quarters of the counties using electronic devices, fewer than 70 percent of the voters voted on the bond issue, whereas in only 15 percent of the counties using all paper ballots did the bond vote fall below 70 percent of all votes cast. Similarly, in all nine of the "electronic" counties, voting on the banking issue fell below 70 percent; the rate fell below that mark in only 26 percent of the paper ballot counties. This evidence suggests that proponents of the convention were justified in being concerned at the Cook County clerk's attempt to place the constitutional question on voting machines. Such a move would have seriously damaged the chances for passage of the call for a constitutional convention.

[7] John P. White, *Voting Machines and the 1958 Defeat of Constitutional Revision in Michigan.* (Ann Arbor, Institute of Public Administration, University of Michigan, Papers in Public Administration #35, 1960).

V

Election of Convention Delegates

[I am] glad for my children's sake as well as mine that
you are willing to accept that responsibility of rewriting
our constitution.

Congressman Abner Mikva

One of the few issues of the 1968 convention call campaign was the
manner in which delegates would be selected—whether by partisan
or nonpartisan elections. Since it was popularly believed that the
type of election would necessarily condition the nature and product
of the convention, for some persons a positive vote for the convention
call hinged upon some reasonable assurance about the mode of delegate election. "Would you give a stranger the keys to your car without knowing his driving habits?" queried one suburban newspaper.[1]
Nevertheless, voters overwhelmingly approved the convention call,
and solutions to problems of delegate selection were left to the legislature and the courts in the months following the constitutional referendum.

Research on nonpartisan elections suggests that they differ from
partisan elections in a number of ways. These differences are mani-
fested both at the voter level and at the candidate level. But a
weighing of the electoral consequences of different forms of election
was not critical to the determination of the method of delegate
selection by the Illinois legislature. Instead, discussion centered on a
distinction between a "party-dominated" convention (the New York
Model) or a "citizen-dominated" convention (the Maryland Model).
Presumably, nonpartisan delegate elections would create at least the

---

[1]*Suburban Times*, Des Plaines, April 8, 1968.

Electing a Constitution

appearance of a citizen-dominated constitutional convention.[2] But, are they legal?

THE ELECTION DEBATE

The question of whether nonpartisan elections are constitutional or not, was not easily resolved. Legislative debate focused on interpretation of the constitutional requirement that the convention delegates "be elected in the same manner" as state senators. The question was whether this phrase referred only to constitutional provisions, or to statutory provisions in existence as well. If it referred only to constitutional provisions, then nonpartisan election of delegates appeared permissible because the 1870 constitution *did not prohibit* the nonpartisan nomination and election of senators. Candidates for the senate are nominated in political party primary elections and elected as partisans because of statutory regulation. However, an attorney general's opinion issued January 28, 1919, before the 1920–22 constitutional convention, supported the view that "in the same manner" includes all existing statutory requirements as well as relevant constitutional provisions. The opinion stated that "delegates must be nominated and elected in the same manner as Senators, and since Senators are nominated in party primary elections [statutory requirement], delegates must also be nominated in party primary elections."[3]

Two proposals were introduced in the General Assembly: the bipartisan and nonpartisan plans. Both were brought forward by Representative Harold Katz at the special summer session of the legislature preceding the November referendum on the convention call. First to be dropped was the bipartisan plan. Under that method, one delegate candidate would have been slated by each party, creating equal party strength at the convention.[4] Naturally, Republicans opposed the measure on the assumption that a wide-open election would give them a majority of convention delegates. Others felt the bipartisan approach was little better, and potentially worse, than regular partisan elections, since polarization along

[2]See Marvin A. Harder, *Non-partisan Elections: A Political Illusion* (New York: Holt, Rinehart and Winston, Inc., 1958), and J.S. Goodman, Wayne Swanson and Elmer Cornwell, Jr., "Political Recruitment in Four Selection Systems," *The Western Political Quarterly* 23 (1970):94.

[3]Illinois Legislative Council, File 6-607, December 6, 1967.

[4]The bipartisan selection plan was used by New Jersey (1966 constitution) and Connecticut (1965 constitution).

party lines could create an unshakeable stalemate on major constitutional issues. Although a proposal calling for the election of delegates on a nonpartisan basis was approved, fourteen to eight, by the House Election Committee, the house turned down the recommended plan. Opposition came from Southern Illinois Republicans who voted against it and Democrats who did not vote. Proponents argued that the nonpartisan plan was needed to help passage of the convention call referendum in November. John Lewis, a resolute opponent of Con Con, arguing against the bipartisan plan, declared that "the sponsor of the bill let the cat right out of the bag when he said if we pass this, the people will vote for that [the convention]."[5]

The legislature reconvened in December, after the November elections in which voters approved the calling of a constitutional convention. The first item for consideration was the nonpartisan issue. House Bill No. 1 was cosponsored by Democrat Katz and House Speaker Ralph T. Smith, a Republican. At the outset, both political parties were split. The Republican party had developed its suburban/downstate cleavage earlier. Although several of the state's liberal Democrats—Adlai Stevenson III, Paul Simon, and Michael Howlett—publicly advocated a nonpartisan system, most regular organization Democrats favored running delegate candidates under party labels.

The legislature held a New Year background session on the problems inherent in establishing the convention. Speaking against the nonpartisan election plan because it would allegedly destroy the party responsibility required to conduct business were house minority leader Thomas McGloon and Senator Thomas Lyons, both Chicago Democrats. In response, Peter Tomei, an active convention campaign organizer, and Kingman Douglass, cochairman of the ICCC, argued its merits. Douglass pointed out that all the large organizations which had endorsed the convention call, including the Illinois Agricultural Association, the Chicago Bar, and the State Chamber of Commerce, favored nonpartisan elections.

Throughout January, the Democrats continued their unofficial opposition to nonpartisanship. The reasons for this are not entirely clear, since a purely partisan contest would have given the Republicans a majority. Furthermore, the Democrats had the organizational capacity to withstand nonpartisan elections and control a number of delegates if they desired—an organizational capacity not enjoyed to that degree by the Republicans.

[5]*Chicago Daily News*, December 19, 1968.

Perhaps the Democrats feared intraparty rivalry from maverick Democrats, believing that nonpartisan elections would invite greater numbers of candidates from groups that had supported dissident Democrats Robert Kennedy and Eugene McCarthy before the presidential convention. Yet experience had shown that machine Democrats were seldom confused in the decades during which nonpartisan elections were used for Chicago aldermanic races. In fact, the liberal forces of the Democratic party did intend to use the delegate elections issue to their own ends. However, on the very day scheduled for the liberal-Democratic study group dinner, Mayor Daley's Democratic leaders in the legislature threw their support behind the nonpartisan plan, thus destroying the immediate threat of a split in the party.[6] The *Chicago Tribune* had earlier predicted the Democratic shift on this issue because the great majority of labor leaders had recently come out for the nonpartisan system. When asked at a press conference whether he believed nonpartisan elections would produce the best results at the convention, Mayor Daley replied, "It all depends on who the delegates are."[7]

THE NOMINATION DEBATE

The electoral process has built into it the means to adjust candidates' chances long before the voter casts his lot. The house and senate agreed on a nonpartisan election, but on little else. In mid-April, the house voted 141 to 0 to approve the senate-passed bill, but only as amended to conform basically with the house's own version approved earlier. The issues, which were eventually resolved in conference committee, were: (a) whether nomination should be by direct primary rather than by party caucus, and (b) whether the election responsibilities of the secretary of state, a Democrat, should be shifted to the governor, a Republican.

The Democrats were solidly opposed, for a number of reasons, to both the party caucus method of nomination—independents would file petitions for nomination—and the transfer of election responsibilities. Proponents of the caucus method argued that it would save the state $2.5 million in election expenses. In addition, a primary would double campaign expenses for hopeful delegates. However, the Democrats argued that the caucus would increase the possibility of party control of delegates—meaning Republican control; either

[6]*Chicago Sun-Times*, February 19, 1969.
[7]*Chicago Tribune*, March 1, 1969.

way, the role of the Democratic party, especially in Cook County, would be little altered.

It was also feared that, with the party caucus method, the convention might include significant numbers of volatile delegates who would represent only a fraction of their areas. Democratic Senator Alan Dixon of Belleville pointed up this danger of the single election system. In a field of perhaps dozens of candidates, well-financed and highly vocal minority groups—"John Birchers and every right and left wing nut in this state"[8]—could elect delegates with as little as 20 percent of the vote. Such groups might be able to nominate a candidate or two under the primary plan, but in a general election with a narrowed field of candidates they would have to appeal to a wider range of people within their district.[9]

The issue of whether or not to transfer responsibilities from the secretary of state to the governor during this special election period was clearer cut. Democrats, of course, wanted to retain such authority with the secretary of state, for he was a Democrat. Republicans wished to transfer this responsibility to the Republican governor. Each party claimed the other would gain an advantage if election matters were in the hands of a Republican or a Democrat. These suspicions were not altogether unjustified, as later became apparent.

By late spring, a conference committee of representatives and senators had ironed out differences in the nonpartisan election requirements for delegate candidates. The compromise plan, Senate Bill 193, subsequently adopted by both houses of the legislature and signed into law by the governor, provided for a primary election on September 23 and a general election on November 18. Delegates would be elected on a nonpartisan basis and all public officials, including legislators, would be eligible to serve in the convention. Four candidates would be nominated in the primary in each of the fifty-eight senatorial districts; two of these would ultimately be chosen in the November general election. No primary would be held if four or fewer candidates filed nominating petitions. (This occurred in only eight of the fifty-eight districts—seven Chicago districts and the 45th district of Peoria.) The position of names on the ballot was to be determined by the order in which petitions were filed with the secretary of state's office. Petitions would need at least 1,000 signatures.

[8]*Chicago Sun-Times,* January 30, 1969.
[9]*Champaign-Urbana Courier,* February 4, 1969.

A "friendly suit" testing the constitutionality of the law's provisions was immediately submitted to the courts by James T. Otis of the Constitution Study Commission. The sections considered controversial were the provision for nonpartisan elections and the eligibility of members of the General Assembly and other elective and appointive offices to serve as members of the constitutional convention without compensation other than expenses. The latter provision raised the question of holding dual office. It was argued that the separation of powers doctrine, Article III of the 1870 constitution, precluded legislators from serving in another governmental body. More explicitly, Article IV, Sec. 3 stated that any person holding any lucrative office under the United States government or the state government should not share a seat in the General Assembly. That is, a legislator would have to resign from the General Assembly if he were elected a delegate.

There were two countervailing arguments. First, it was put forward that the constitutional restrictions in Article IV pertained to legislators and not to delegates. As for the delegates, they must possess the same "qualifications" as senators, but they were not subject to the same "disqualifications."[10]

The second and more persuasive argument was in the nature of precedent. Although an attorney general's opinion (March 1, 1919, since lost) stated that a legislator must resign his seat upon election as a convention delegate, only one of six legislators in the 1920-22 constitutional convention actually did so.[11] In fact, two were re-elected to the General Assembly during their terms as delegates and were duly seated, for each house of the General Assembly under Article IV, Sec. 9, had the right to judge the election, the returns, and the qualifications of its members, despite the 1919 attorney general's opinion.

A split Illinois Supreme Court[12] upheld the legislative enactment for eligibility and election of constitutional convention delegates. Nevertheless, Senator Russell Arrington, president pro tempore and majority leader of the state senate, withdrew his name as a candidate for convention delegate at that time. In a prepared statement issued on July 14, 1969, Arrington disagreed with the majority of the court, saying he believed that "a State legislator is prohibited by our present constitution from serving as a delegate."[13] Perhaps the

[10]Illinois Legislative Council, File 5-987, January 3, 1967.
[11]Illinois Legislative Council, File 6-409, October 6, 1967.
[12]Supreme Court Justices Schaeffer and Ward dissented.
[13]Statement by Senator W. Russell Arrington, Springfield, July 14, 1969, mimeo.

greatest barrier to his delegate candidacy was the fact that Governor Ogilvie's one-year budget proposal required that the legislature return for another session in the spring of 1970. Since the constitutional convention would have convened by that time, Arrington probably felt that such a conflict was best avoided. It was conjectured by at least one editorial writer that Arrington wished to avoid another possible conflict. John Dreiske of the *Chicago Sun-Times* wrote,

> The other reason for his withdrawal as a candidate could very well, some close to Arrington believe, have been that his election as a delegate would have provoked a political fight for president of the convention. . . . Arrington is particular anathema to State Rep. Paul F. Elward (D–Chicago), unofficial aid to House Minority leader. If Arrington were elected a delegate and Elward, a candidate, were to make it too, there would have been one of the fanciest little knockdown and dragouts for the presidency that you would ever want to see. . . . [Arrington] would not have passed up doing his best to make sure that Elward not achieve parliamentary control of the constitutional convention. . . . However, with Arrington out of the picture, there is not expected to be any fur-flying battle for the presidency. The prospects are for quiet dignity to prevail and NO POLITICS.[14]

Five Illinois legislators did remain in the race for delegate to the constitutional convention.

THE BALLOT POSITION CONTROVERSY

Joseph Harris has noted the importance of ballot position, commenting that it is "not at all flattering to the intelligence of the American voter that the position at the top of a list of candidates is of material help to the candidates thus favored."[15] While this statement may not be altogether accurate, at least it can be assumed that no one will *lose* any votes as the result of being at the top of the ballot. In the case of election of delegates to the constitutional convention, since the election was to be nonpartisan—which meant that there would be no party labels to guide the voters—many politicians and would-be candidates believed that the voters would simply start at the top of the ballot and mark the first two names.

Several methods can be used to determine ballot position: discretionary, alphabetical, rotation, drawing of lots, and order of filing.

[14]*Chicago Sun-Times*, September 8, 1969.
[15]Joseph P. Harris, *Election Administration in the United States* (Washington, D.C.: The Brookings Institution, 1934), p. 24.

In some states, electoral law allows the proper state officials to determine the arrangement of names on the ballot. Where discretion is permitted, officers usually arrange the ballot so as to favor their own party or faction. One observer has declared that in Chicago the power to arrange the order of the party columns on the general election ballot is one of the things that gives a 50,000 vote advantage to the party that controls the election machinery. In other states, official discretion is completely removed by the rule that candidates' names shall appear in alphabetical order. Even under this system, however, factions and parties have attempted to gain an advantage by selecting candidates whose names stand at the beginning of the alphabet. Obviously, the Wilsons and the Zablonskis of electoral politics do not usually favor such a system.

The rotation method is carried out as follows: Several ballot forms are printed, and the candidates or party whose name appears at the top (or at the left-hand side) of the first form is moved to the bottom (or right-hand side) on the second form, and each other candidate moves up (or to the left) one position. This procedure is repeated until as many forms have been printed as there are candidates or parties, so that each of these appears in each position on one group of ballots. This supposedly neutral or objective method is not, however, without disadvantages. For example, the system works against the candidate or party wishing to advertise position on the ballot in an appeal to semiliterate voters.

The lottery is an attempt to maintain the ballot neutrality of rotation but utilizes a far simpler procedure. The disadvantages of rotation are also avoided.

Order of filing was the method to be used in the Illinois convention delegate elections. Candidates would be listed on the ballot in the order in which they filed for the election. This is an imperfect way of circumventing favoritism by election officials, since the procedures for receiving filing fees or declarations of candidacy do not always incorporate safeguards against collusion between a candidate and the election officers. Political observers have noted the negative results of the system, such as dishonest jockeying by some of the candidates, and the undignified scramble in front of the office of the secretary of state several days before the filing date.

The Democrats, headed by Chicago's Mayor Daley, favored a system which would allow Democratic Secretary of State Paul Powell, to list candidates on the ballot in the order in which they filed their nominating petitions. Republicans, however, feared Democratic treachery under such a system. As an alternative proposal, Republicans favored a lottery system in which the names of the candidates would be coded on slips of paper, placed in a hat, and then drawn by either Governor Richard B. Ogilvie or someone he designated as his official representative. The Democrats countered this proposal on three fronts. First they argued that the governor was a Republican and hence they feared Republican treachery. Second, they pointed out that the secretary of state's office is the official election agency of the state. Third, they stressed the constitutional provision which stated that delegates to a constitutional convention are to be elected "in the same manner as members of the Illinois Senate," and, since there is no lottery system for the placement of senate candidates on the ballot, it was felt the same should hold true for the delegate election.

Eventually the Democrats won the fight over ballot position, and the stage was set for heated political battle. By July 7, 1969, the first day to file petitions, almost 300 candidates had received the required 1,000 signatures on their nominating petitions. At 8 a.m. on that Monday there were approximately 100 people in front of the secretary of state's office. These candidates had waited throughout the night to file on the first day of the five-day filing period, seeking the top position on their district's ballot. With nerves on edge after the night-long vigil, some candidates became rather unruly when they noticed a state official carrying boxes of petitions through a side door. The candidates charged the employee on his third trip and knocked the box from his arms, scattering the petitions. After summoning police to restore order, Don Ed, head of the Index Division under Secretary Powell, explained that those petitions that had been mailed would receive first priority. He then produced a form letter issued by his office to candidates noting that petitions received in Monday morning's mail would be processed before those delivered in person. Ed defended this procedure by claiming, "This is a long-standing practice in [petition] filings of this kind." Rejecting the notion that tradition takes precedence over justice and noting that Mayor Daley's son and other important Democrats had received the preferred ballot positions, two Chicago candidates, Bernard Weisberg and Mary Lee Leahy, filed suits charging Secretary of State Powell with favoritism in the ballot placement of candidates' names. Weisberg, a general counsel for the American Civil Liberties Union, filed his suit in the United States District Court in Chicago on behalf of all candidates that he said were victimized by Powell's arbitrary and discriminatory policy in placing the names on the official ballot. He accused Powell of notifying regular party organizations, both Democratic and Republican, that preferential treatment would be given persons other than those delivering petitions in person. He asked the court to issue a preliminary and permanent injunction restraining Powell from certifying the order of placement until ballot position was determined by lot or by some other fair method. The second suit, filed in Sangamon County Court by Mary Lee Leahy, a Chicago attorney, also challenged Powell's procedure in listing candidates on the ballot. "Unless the court intervenes to insure fair elections, public confidence in the constitutional convention will be undermined and the success of the convention will be jeopardized," said Mrs. Leahy.[16] She then said that Powell had acted in a discriminatory manner in giving top ballot positions to Chicago candidates who had been endorsed by the Chicago Democratic Party.

Secretary of State Powell noted that the practice has been used for at least fifty years. He continued, "If we handled them the way some of these rabble-rousers wanted, folks would be hiring some Chicago Bear bruisers to knock everybody else down so they'd be the first in line . . . and we'd end up with a line from here [Champaign County Fair] to Chicago."[17] Powell said the law required him to place names on the ballot in the order they were received. He said nothing required him to give preference to candidates who presented their petitions in person over those who mailed them.

On Monday, July 15, Judge Joseph Sam Perry of the United States District Court issued a temporary order restraining Powell from assigning positions or certifying ballots. On July 23, in Sangamon County Circuit Court in Springfield, Judge William Chamberlain ruled that Chicago attorney Mary Lee Leahy had failed to show the need for an immediate injunction against Secretary of State Powell and dismissed Mrs. Leahy's suit challenging the secretary of state's practices in listing delegates' names on the ballot. According to the court's ruling,

> The evidence . . . can lead to no other conclusion than the candidates were in fact listed in the order that they were filed. The evidence showed that the Monday morning mail was received by the Secretary of State's office late Sunday. Obviously, a preferred candidate's petitions are filed first, and, as a result, gets the preferred listing. Again which petitions are first filed is an administrative decision.[18]

[16]*Champaign-Urbana News Gazette,* July 9, 1969.
[17]*Champaign-Urbana Courier,* July 23, 1969.
[18]Judge Chamberlain's ruling in the Leahy suit on July 23, 1969.

The next day Mrs. Leahy chastised Judge Chamberlain for failing to disqualify himself before hearing the suit. The basis for her statement was the alleged close relationship between Judge Chamberlain and Secretary of State Powell. The Illinois Blue Book of 1959–60 listed Chamberlain as "legal secretary to the Speaker of the House," who was Paul Powell. In addition, the Blue Book of 1963–64 identified Chamberlain as Powell's legal advisor. Further, he had been Powell's immediate predecessor in the office of secretary of state.

In the Weisberg case, Judge Perry withdrew the temporary order keeping Secretary of State Paul Powell from certifying the ballot position of candidates for the constitutional convention. Eight days later, however, the United States Court of Appeals ordered Powell to discard a "discriminatory" ballot listing of candidates. After hearing Powell admit that he gave favored treatment to candidates whose names he recognized, the court said Powell "arranged the names of candidates whose petitions were delivered by mail according to his own personal preference and on the basis of affiliation with the two major parties." In addition, Powell apparently advised candidates "on a selective basis" as to the advantage of mailing their petitions to him. The three judge panel, consisting of Luther M. Swygert, Thomas E. Fairchild, and Walter J. Cummings, ordered Powell to pursue the following system in determining ballot position:

1. Petitions filed in person and stamped with the time and date will remain in the relative order in which they were accepted.
2. Mailed petitions will be inserted among personally delivered petitions on a random basis.
3. At a public drawing, a ballot position number will be drawn for each petition.

Secretary of State Powell did not accept this decision and immediately released a statement which read in part:

> The Federal Court of Appeals suggestion the other day to conduct a lottery regarding candidates listing on the constitutional ballot is more far-reaching in its effect than merely this one election. It not only will affect elections within this state for years to come . . . but if this suggestion of a lottery stands, it usurps the constitutional authority of state government. The conduct of elections is a prerogative of the legislature and not the courts. I took an oath of office to uphold the Illinois Constitution and I will never renege on that oath.[19]

[19]*Chicago Tribune,* August 10, 1969.

While the secretary of state was embroiled with the courts, the state electoral board, composed of Governor Ogilvie, State Auditor Michael Howlett, Secretary of State Powell, Attorney General William Scott, Democratic State Chairman James Ronan, and Republican State Chairman Victor Smith, delayed certifying the ballot for the election until attorneys for Powell had time to petition to vacate the court's ruling. It was at this time that Powell, as part of his defense, admitted that he gave top ballot positions to major party acquaintances, mostly Democrats, because he wanted to "make sure that some long-haired Communist was not in first place."[20] The Court of Appeals did not accept this argument, and refused to vacate their earlier decision.

On Tuesday, August 12, the state electoral board agreed to comply with the court's order to hold a lottery and to certify the ballot. In so doing the board saved the election structure; under the timetable for elections in Illinois, unless the county clerks had received the certified ballots by midnight August 12, the whole structure of elections for convention delegates would have been destroyed since the primary could not have been held on September 23 as required by the enabling legislation.

Ultimately, ballot position in the primary campaign turned out to have only a marginal effect on the election outcome. Of all the candidates whose names were drawn first in the lottery, 43.4 percent failed to finish among the top four. Figures for those in the second, third, and fourth spots who failed to finish among the top four were 47.8 percent, 39.1 percent, and 45.6 percent, respectively.

More significant than ballot position was an effective campaign. In fact, what strength and resources candidates had put together during the eliminating round at the September primary was to have an influence upon their successful bid in November. A hard primary run which secured a first or second ballot position in the November election was an important advantage. Similarly, an early, well-organized and well-financed campaign left little at the final stage but for a candidacy to gain momentum. It is not surprising that in half of the senatorial districts, *both* the first and second place candidates won.

The Delegate Campaign

For a number of delegates, the political parties had little influence upon their decision to seek nomination. In the main, therefore, parties were not *initially* involved in candidate selection. Of sixty-

[20]*Chicago Sun-Times*, August 12, 1969.

TABLE I. CANDIDATE DISTRIBUTION AND ELIMINATION

Area	Sept. 23 Candidates	Nov. 18 Candidates	Delegates
Suburban Cook	104	36	18
Chicago	138	77	42
Downstate	259	112	56
Total	501[21]	225	116

Source: *Illinois Political Reporter* 9, no. 3, (September 1969).

nine respondents to one delegate poll,[22] forty-seven were self-recruited while twenty-two were encouraged by groups to enter the qualifying primary. However, the majority of these recruiting groups were ad hoc, unorganized instruments, representing for the major part friends and associates of the delegate. The principal recruiting groups of the formal type were the Cook County Democratic and Republican parties and the Farm Bureau. Approximately two-thirds of the self-recruited delegates had worked in some capacity on the convention call campaign in 1968, and they overwhelmingly believed this experience had been of benefit to them in their bids. Its significance was measured in terms of prior contacts, potential sources for support, and a general background in constitutional matters which served as a positive campaign aid.

For most respondents, the political parties became noticeably involved in their campaigns, if at all, only after the qualifying primary—with the exception of the preprimary activity of the Chicago parties, which had been active early recruiters. Local party organizations were probably reluctant to endorse individuals in such widely contested elections, first, because selective endorsing might well have split organizations internally and, second, because endorsements in a primary boasting ten, twelve, or more candidates (the highest number was eighteen in suburban Cook County 6th District) would have been less effective because of the nature of the minimal support strategy in which 15 to 20 percent of the vote was for many sufficient to qualify for a position on the November ballot. It was not inconceivable that a candidate might not be able to pinpoint every vote cast for him. Close candidate-elector relationships significantly replace the role of party in such contests.

[21]Actually 495 candidates remained on the primary ballot after the period of withdrawal.
[22]Conducted by the author and referred to throughout this chapter. The greater number of nonrespondents to this poll were recruited and endorsed by the Democratic party which dilutes the above observation.

Of the sixty-nine respondents to the delegate poll, fifty-one eventually received political party endorsements (another source claims that roughly 100 of the 116 delegates to the convention had been party endorsed[23]); 69 percent of all party endorsees were interviewed by local party committees. The remaining endorsees who had not been previously interviewed were overwhelmingly Republican. The Cook County Republican party was likely to endorse dissident Democrats or independents who faced organizational competition in the general election. Hence, many of these endorsements were perfunctory at best. In a majority of cases, the political parties did not fulfill for candidates the traditional roles of campaign organizer or money raiser.

Overwhelmingly, candidates either were self-financed or acquired financial support from individuals, not from groups or formal organizations, including parties. The average amount expended per candidacy (including both primary and general election) was $4,800. The range extended from $100 to $25,000. A breakdown of primary versus general election expenses indicates that 62 percent spent less in the primary, 30 percent spent equal amounts in both elections, and 8 percent spent more in the primary. While independent candidates spent considerably more on their campaigns than the average amount cited above and those candidates challenging Cook County Democratic endorsees exceeded $9,000 on the average, it was not money that made the difference in most campaigns. Other factors played crucial roles, the most important of which were the volunteer nature of citizens' campaign groups and the number and type of local endorsements.

Local newspaper endorsements undeniably contributed to successful candidacies. All but six of the sixty-nine respondents to the delegate poll had press support. Approximately two-thirds of those endorsed for the primary in forty-one districts by both the *Chicago Tribune* and *Chicago Sun-Times* were elected delegates to the constitutional convention.[24] The importance of the press in these campaigns was accentuated by the relatively little interest taken in the delegate elections by the electronic media. Television and radio producers alike complained that it would have been impossible to grant equal time, as required by the Federal Communications Commission, to the great numbers of candidates running in these elections. The media also avoided general public service announcements

[23]*The Illinois Political Reporter* 9, no. 2, (August 1969).

[24]*Chicago Sun-Times*, September 22, 1969, and *Chicago Tribune*, September 22, 1969.

about the nature and importance of delegate selection: that voters should exercise their franchise on such-and-such dates. The press was the only outlet for many candidates with little or no media funds, and it remained for many voters the only source of information in elections without party labels.

Many special interest organizations endorsed candidates for the general election, although few contributed to the campaign caches or manpower needs of the candidates. The most active came from the Farm Bureau in the central and southern regions of the state and the Independent Voters of Illinois in the Chicago metropolitan area and adjacent communities. Other major endorsing organizations were the Committee on Political Education (an arm of the AFL-CIO), the State Chamber of Commerce, and the Better Government Association (BGA). The BGA supported approximately 80 percent of Chicago metropolitan area delegates (partisan and independent.)[25]

DELEGATE CAMPAIGN ORGANIZATIONS

Although campaign styles and organization varied with the individual and the nature of the district, a loosely-knit format generally prevailed. Campaign organizations could be described in four general categories: party-formal; formal; semiformal; and informal. Local political parties made available to some candidates their precinct organizations and officers; these were the "party-formal" organizations. The "formal" organizations were not party sponsored, but candidates opened official headquarters and hired staff which included office and campaign managers and public relations firms. The "semiformal" organizations commonly possessed citizens' committees with varying types of campaign network throughout the district. For example, several delegates employed telephone brigades; others set up committee appendages in the major population centers; and one delegate specifically organized a system of groups which had direct appeal to major voting blocs in the district. The citizens' committees themselves varied in amounts of campaign activity in which they engaged. Perhaps the most active delegate campaigns were those of Peter Tomei and Mary Lee Leahy. Thus roughly 350 canvassers covered 190 of the 207 precincts in Tomei's Chicago district one week before the election. Generally, all Chicago independents pursued active campaigns.

[25] *Chicago Daily News*, September 9, 1969.

The "informal" or unstructured campaigns were home based, with the candidates and immediate friends formulating what little campaign strategy existed. The breakdown of campaign organization described by sixty-nine respondents was: party-formal, 17 percent (twelve);[26] formal, 6 percent (four); semiformal, 42 percent (twenty-nine); and informal, 30 percent (twenty-one); the type of campaign organization was not ascertained for 5 percent (three). Naturally, the formal type of campaign organization was least common because of its overall expense. Outside the party-formal type of organization in which cost was borne by the political party, campaign organization clearly paralleled reported campaign expenses, with the less expensive campaigns utilizing the home-based or informal campaign techniques.

PARTISAN V. NONPARTISAN ELECTION

The question remains whether a partisan contest would have produced different contenders and ultimately different convention delegates. In the poll of delegates a majority of respondents said they believed that the election results would indeed have been different in a partisan contest. However, an only slightly smaller number felt that the results in their districts would not have been at all different, either because the candidates were supported and endorsed by a party and hence the contest appeared to be partisan, or because in some districts that were strong one-party areas the candidates who acknowledged their majority party position faced little danger of defeat.

Neither political party gained or lost footing within comparable electoral areas in the nonpartisan elections for convention delegates. Altogether, nineteen of fifty districts (eight districts belonged to neither party) were affected in terms of electing either an independent or a political opposite in traditionally one-party areas. Although both "strong" and "weak" party areas were equally affected (nine and ten districts respectively), the "strong" one-party districts gave up fewer delegates—one per district—as would be expected. On the other hand, several "weak" one-party districts gave up both delegates to the minority party or to independents; this amounted to a 40 percent political turnover in Republican districts and a 61 percent turnover in Democratic areas.

[26]Not included in this figure are a number of Democratic party-endorsed delegates from Chicago who did not respond to this questionnaire.

TABLE II. EFFECT OF NONPARTISAN ELECTION

Party Strength[27]	Districts	Potential Delegates	Actual Number of Delegates	Delegate Net Loss
Strong				
Rep.	20	40	34	6 (15%)
Dem.	13	26	24	2 (8%)
Weak				
Rep.	8	16	9	7 (40%)
Dem.	9	18	7	11 (61%)
Swing (and Modi-fied)[28]	8	16	NA	NA
Totals	58	116	NA	26
Rep.	28	56	43	13
Dem.	22	44	31	13
Swing	8	16	—[29]	NA

Probably the most noticeable political shifts occurred in suburban Cook County, a Republican stronghold, which comprises nine senatorial (convention delegate) districts. Of the eighteen delegates from these districts, six, or one-third, were either Democrats or independents. However, Republicans picked up delegates in less strong downstate Democratic areas and in the marginal areas. They had no impact upon Democratic districts within the city of Chicago, where elections were lost only to independents.

Despite the party labels, the question remains whether the delegates as individuals varied philosophically or otherwise from the types of delegates who would have been elected under party auspices. One can only speculate. A number, but by no means a majority, of delegates felt that as independents they would not have been elected. Similarly, a somewhat larger group had not been pre-

[27]Key: Strong - A district which elected state senators of the same party in both 1966 and 1970.

Weak - A district combining one substantial party victory and one marginal (less than 10 percent) election.

Swing - A district in which senatorial elections in 1966 and 1970 were decided with less than a 10 percent margin.

[28]Two districts are not actually "swing" areas politically because the plurality margins exceeded 10 percent. However, these districts swung from "weak" Republican areas to "weak" Democratic areas within the four years considered.

[29]The Republicans gained more often from the swing districts than did Democrats (principally because the majority had swung from marginal Republican in 1966 to marginal Democrat in 1970). The 1970 election is generally accepted as unique for its number of Democratic successes. Three other districts although swing areas, returned Republican senators in both the 1966 and 1970 elections.

viously involved in partisan matters and wished to create an image
of party sympathizer but not of party "hack." In fact, a large
minority of delegates, 48 of 116, claimed no previous political experience whatsoever; not only had they not run for any office
before, they had done no party organizational work (e.g., precinct
captains, etc.) either.[30] What emerges, in effect, are groups of
amateur Republicans and Democrats and some independents counterbalanced by an equal number of political professionals from both
parties. For this reason alone, convention behavior retained a
fluidity which could not have developed under strict partisanship.
Many delegates felt a sense of political independence which does not
exist to any like degree among party professionals. Nevertheless, a
statistical analysis of roll calls at the convention revealed that the
best explanation for roll call voting behavior was party affiliation.[31]

Generally, arguments for nonpartisan delegate elections have
rested upon some concept of a "people's" rather than a "party-
dominated" constitutional convention. The Second Constitution
Study Commission endorsed nonpartisanship on the basis that the
public strongly distrusted conventional party politics—that a
"political" constitution would have only a slight chance for approval
by the electorate. However, a survey after the convention call
referendum disclosed that most voters wanted a mixed convention.
When asked what kind of convention delegates they wanted, 18
percent of the respondents said they wanted public officials, 18
percent wanted individuals not associated with government and
politics, 51.5 percent wanted some of both, and 12.5 percent didn't
know.[32]

In effect, the 1970 Illinois Constitutional Convention did fall
somewhere between the two extremes. The fact that party labels did
not appear on the ballot did not hinder broad editorial delineation
of delegates' political persuasion: "Republicans appear to hold
fifty-three seats, Democrats forty-eight and independents fifteen. If
the independents are aligned by primary voting habits, the tally
stands at fifty-six Republicans, and fifty-five Democrats and five
delegates undetermined. . . . No party secured a clear majority in
the convention."[33]

[30] Illinois State Historical Society—Constitution Convention Profiles.

[31] David Kenney, Jack R. Van Der Slik and Samuel J. Pernacciaro, *Roll Call! Patterns of Voting in the Sixth Illinois Constitutional Convention.* (Urbana: University of
Illinois Press, 1974).

[32] Market Opinion Research, *1968 Illinois After Election Study* (Chicago, Illinois,
January 1969). Sample Size: 800

[33] *Chicago Sun-Times,* November 30, 1969.

It is undeniable that some local political party organizations took interest in delegate selection and that their endorsements were often critical. It was a rare candidate who refused party support. However, the wide-open nominating election introduced many new faces to Illinois politics. The large numbers of candidates, coupled with an extremely low primary turnout (average of 18 percent) which allowed candidates to advance a small voter base, threw open the doors to individuals who admitted they would have had little if any chance in a partisan primary, much less a nominating caucus. Although the campaign for election took on a partisan reflection, the parties had to endorse available candidates. In effect, the parties' influence was halved by removing from their control the nominating or eliminating process. Of course, the Cook County Democratic party, as an initial recruiter, maintained unbroken control of a substantial number of candidacies.

Clearly, candidates in a strictly nonpartisan contest also bear some special burdens. In enumerating the general characteristics of nonpartisan elections, Charles Adrian has noted:

> Under the traditional political system, the party carries on much of the financing burden as a staff function. If a candidate can secure organizational backing, he is free to carry on his campaign with little or no worry about the requisite funds: the party has machinery to care for this problem. On the other hand, the nonpartisan candidate is an individual who, when he first enters politics, has no organized support or money-raising mechanism. When he knows that he must spend his own money, or that of friends, or persuade an important interest group to give him aid, the burden of campaigning is made so heavy that the likelihood of an individual's trying to gain a seat is decreased.[34]

Most Illinois residents who made the decision to run for a delegate seat at the constitutional convention had to accept these burdens. Who were these people?

CANDIDATE PROFILES AND IMAGES

Over 500 petitions were filed in the initial phase of delegate selection. Of these candidates, three-quarters were college-educated and two-thirds were professionals (especially lawyers) and businessmen. Ten percent were women and 7 percent were black. From these preliminary 500 candidates, 116 survived the eliminating rounds: 97

[34]Charles Adrian, "General Characteristics of Non-partisan Elections," *American Political Science Review* 46 (1952):772.

delegates were professionals or businessmen and 92 had at least a college degree; 57 had professional or graduate degrees. Black delegates numbered 13 and there were 15 women.

The turnout rates for the delegate primary (18 percent) and general election (27 percent) were low. Although there are few statistics on the types of voters at these two nonpartisan elections, assumptions can be made. As in any election, voters must acquire some information about candidates even if it is no more than a party cue. In a nonpartisan election, party cues are beneficial to voters, although they still have the burden of having to remember the candidate's name, since the party label will not be on the ballot. More commonly, however, name recognition alone—the politics of acquaintance—predominates. Controversial issues are avoided. Instead, candidates depend upon family names, ethnic identification, or secondary group association. Respondents to the delegate campaign poll cited these factors most often as their greatest campaign assets.

More important than the cues are the means by which these distinctions between candidates are made available to voters. The least effective means are the candidates' own attempts to disseminate information. The main sources of information are the press and civic, social, and professional associations. This raises the question of socioeconomic class and voting patterns. Behavior studies have categorized news readership according to class-oriented interests. It is unlikely that a large segment of even the newspaper-buying population learned anything about the candidates. With the major exception of labor, the lower socioeconomic groups report fewer organizational memberships. Because these groups lack a major source for election information such as organizational newsletters, lines of communication produced by the press and secondary associations disproportionately reach the upper and middle classes.

A study of voter participation and degree of voter information,[35] shows that a lack of generalized voter education reduces voter participation generally and potential lower class participation specifically. Voters without adequate information are unable to perceive differences between candidates. Lacking a means to distinguish between individuals on the ballot, the (even remotely) rational voter will stay home on election day. Table III shows the effect of this process on the election of delegates to Con Con. The study from which these findings emerged reveals further that, if the populace is

---

[35] Oliver Walter, "The 1969 Illinois Constitutional Convention Delegate Election and Voter Rationality," (Ph.D. dissertation, University of Illinois, 1972).

divided on the basis of perceived differences among the candidates, the upper one-fourth will have a higher percentage of Republicans, have a higher social status, have a higher educational attainment, be more effective and involved in the community, and have a higher sense of social duty and general political knowledge than the lower three-fourths.

TABLE III. VOTER PARTICIPATION AT DELEGATE ELECTION AND PERCEIVED CANDIDATE DIFFERENCE

Did you vote?	10th (Chicago) PCD Index*			
	Low 1	2	3	High 4
Yes	17.6	51.5	72.3	70.9
No	82.4	48.5	27.7	29.1
	100.0	100.0	100.0	100.0
	N = (34)	(33)	(47)	(55)
	47th (Champaign-Urbana)			
Yes	20.6	44.1	54.5	66.7
No	79.4	55.9	45.5	33.3
	100.0	100.0	100.0	100.0
	N = (102)	(34)	(33)	(36)

*The perceived candidate difference index (PCD) used here was created from the twenty-eight questions in which the respondent was asked to estimate candidate positions. Twenty-five of these questions dealt with issues deemed most important in the campaign and the remaining three had to do with the partisan affiliation of those running for office.

With important exceptions, we may assume, since the voter turnout was 18 percent in the primary and 27 percent in the general election, that the delegates to the constitutional convention were characteristically upper-middle class and, given the available evidence, that the majority of voters involved in delegate selection were probably middle class as well.

VI

The Ballot Battle

Probably the most decisive session of the convention.
Samuel Witwer

By mid-August 1970, the work of the convention was drawing to a close. Two important questions remained to be settled—the structure of the ballot to be submitted to the voters and the date of the referendum. Ballot logistics, especially, were the focus of what were perhaps the most intensive maneuverings and certainly the most dramatic of the convention's deliberations.

The recent failures to ratify constitutions in Maryland, Rhode Island, and New York hung like dark clouds over Illinois Con Con delegates. From almost the outset, many of them were wondering about how their completed work might be submitted to the electorate. Because specific controversial items in the proposed constitution had the potential of bringing down the entire house, delegates sought to submit some of the more controversial items to the voters separately. The hope was that the main document could be saved even if some of the separate questions failed. The record in other states sustained that hope. Of fifteen attempts to revise state constitutions significantly in the period from 1963 to 1970, eight were successful and seven were not. All seven of the unsuccessful attempts had been presented to the voters as a single package, whereas seven of the eight that were successful were submitted as separate items (the one exception was Michigan).

Thus a number of the substantive committees of the Illinois convention, at one time or another, considered the separate submission of some portion of their constitutional article. However, the fact that the revenue committee decided to retain its total revenue article as a

64

part of the main package shows clearly that not *all* controversial items were submitted separately to the voters; in fact, even *the most controversial* items were not cut out of the proposed constitution. However, four items did ultimately reach the voters separated from the main body of the proposed constitution. These were the issues of: legislative representation in the lower house; judicial selection; abolition of the death penalty; and the eighteen-year-old vote.

THE SEPARATE SUBMISSIONS STORY

Two issues in particular, the election of representatives to the state House of Representatives and the method of judicial selection, indicate the special problems facing delegates to the convention and the kinds of solutions that were attempted. The story of their eventual separate submission illustrates the effect of Democratic party cohesiveness at this convention and the difficulty of achieving compromises on certain issues.

As the convention neared the end of its task, only two realistic alternatives appeared possible on the issue of electing representatives to the state House of Representatives: one called for single-member districts while the other called for multi-member (in this case, three-member) districts with a provision for cumulative voting. Under this provision, first introduced to Illinois through the 1870 constitution and now unique to this state, the voter can cast one vote for each candidate, one and half votes for each of two candidates, or all three votes for one candidate. Cumulative voting has enabled the Democratic party to achieve political representation in downstate districts which normally would elect only Republicans. Naturally, most Democrats at the convention (but not all) favored this alternative.

Proponents of legislative change had prevailed on both first and second readings. Included in the document, at that stage, was the proviso for single-member districts and the abolition of cumulative voting. However, during second reading, convention delegates voted to submit a separate proposal to the voters calling for the retention of multi-member districts and cumulative voting but with the stipulation that each political party be required to nominate no fewer than two candidates in each district thereby guaranteeing competition. Despite the appearance of compromise, the advantage clearly rested with those who could get their proposal on the ballot as an integral part of the constitution rather than as a separate proposal. By the third reading, therefore, the battleground on this issue shifted to the concern over ballot format.

Deliberation on the manner of judicial selection had also broken down to two alternatives: election versus the merit selection or appointment of judges. The election of judges, the then current practice, was clearly favored by Chicago Mayor Daley and his convention representatives as well as a number of downstate delegates who feared domination by the Chicago Bar in any appointment process. Unlike the proponents for legislative changes, who were able to retain their position in the main document through second reading, supporters of merit selection of judges were to witness their early coalition collapse. Not only was there a vote trade-off by Chicago Democrats, there was also an increasing unwillingness on the part of merit selection enthusiasts to compromise what they believed to be necessary reform at *all* levels. The compromise, coming out of first reading, had called for appointment of judges at supreme and apellate levels and continued election of district judges. A second reading amendment proposed by Helen Kinney, Republican member of the judiciary committee, was endorsed by the convention in one of several second reading turnabouts. The approved Kinney amendment called for the election of all judges with nomination by petition at primary elections (rather than nomination by the prevailing party convention). The appointment of the Illinois judiciary at all levels was then approved for separate submission. The earlier plan to appoint some judges and elect others had disappeared.

The issues, now swept clear of compromise, were unambiguous. Both sides on both issues had one single goal: to get their position into the main document for submission to the voters while leaving the alternative isolated as a separate proposal for separate submission.

THE BALLOT FORMAT

The structure of the ballot generated constitutional controversy as well as political controversy. At the heart of the constitutional dilemma was the provision of the 1870 constitution requiring a majority of those voting for all revisions. However, in a situation such as that presented by the alternatives for legislative representation and judicial selection, where in each case one was part of the main package and the other was to be submitted as a separate proposition, the constitutional provision fails to set a standard for victory. For example, while the main package—containing the provision for election of judges—might be approved, the voters might "also approve" the separately submitted plan for appointment of judges. Which would prevail? On what terms? There were three politically feasible options for such separate items. Each had to achieve: (1) more votes than the main document, (2) a majority of those voting at the election, or (3) merely a majority of those voting on the issue regardless of the vote on the main document or at the election. (In any case, the main package would have to pass.) Delegate response to these alternatives depended on whether they supported or opposed the items which were outside the constitution. As it turned out, the question was moot.

One day before the convention was to meet for third reading, President Witwer proposed a new alternative to the Committee on Style, Drafting and Submission. He suggested that *both* alternatives for legislative and judicial selection be placed outside the proposed constitution as amendments to the 1870 constitution or to the new constitution if this document were approved. The suggestion met with little enthusiasm. Revisionists and standpatters had each scored a partial victory on second reading and were uncertain about the electoral advantages or disadvantages of the new proposal in relation to their own preferred alternatives.

Witwer's proposal was shunted aside and the third reading proceeded fairly routinely. Each article was reaffirmed and enrolled in the new constitution until the final presentation of the legislative article. By that time, a new coalition had been forged. It included some Republicans under the banner of President Witwer, independents who had always been lukewarm to single-member districts, and Chicago Democrats. The product of this emergent faction was a switch in position on the two representational formulas. For the first time in the course of the 1970 convention, the multi-member districts with cumulative voting were put into the constitution. A victory for Chicago Democrats! Not quite. The session was adjourned before the entire legislative article received final pro forma approval. The following morning, in what was expected to be a routine vote for enrollment, the legislative article failed to receive the necessary fifty-nine votes. Absent from this crucial roll call were a number of Democrats who had perhaps celebrated their victory of the previous day too soon and too long.

The dramatic, almost bewildering, climax . . . seemed to come unheralded, with no warning, with no portents of an approaching storm. It followed almost immediately upon a stunning convention reversal the evening before on the issue of single-member versus multi-member legislative districts coupled with cumulative voting, . . . Hard won political victories of the Chicago Democrats, which placed the provisions for elected judges and multi-member legislative districts with cumulative voting in the main document of the constitution, were completely undone.[1]

Any amendments to the proposed constitution now required a suspension of the rules—with a two-thirds vote. After lengthy and heated debate, a suspension was approved for consideration of an amendment offered by Democrat Betty Ann Keegan, Republican Lewis Wilson, and independent Wayne Whalen. It deleted from the main document all provisions pertaining to the nature of legislative districts and the method of selecting judges and placed both alternatives for both issues in separate submission proposals. After seven hours of intense debate, the amendment was approved, seventy to thirty-nine. Like the separate proposals on the death penalty and the eighteen-year-old vote, it was thought that the electorate would now be given a clear choice of alternatives without a built-in advantage for any one alternative.

The amendment stated that if neither alternative of the two contested issues was approved by the voters, the "applicable provisions" of the 1870 constitution would remain in force. This hinged upon approval of the main document; the reverse or adoption of separately submitted items as amendments to the 1870 constitution, should the proposed constitution fail, never garnered support. In effect, the "applicable provisions" of the 1870 constitution and the alternatives for multi-member legislative districts with cumulative voting and the election of judges were only slightly different. Consequently, the reform options were in fact disadvantaged—a situation perhaps overlooked by the Chicago Democratic organization as it first stared into the face of defeat. It did not go unnoticed for long, however.

Those who had been concerned about a "self-destruct" mechanism in the original ballot structure were especially pleased with the result. Previously, proponents of the separated propositions were placed in the difficult position of voting for both the option they opposed in the main document and their favored proposal in a separate submission. Convention President Witwer feared that these delegates would prevent adoption of the proposed constitution by not casting a vote for the main document and voting only for the separate submission proposals. There was a real possibility that the proposed constitution might not obtain a majority from voters

[1]Rubin G. Cohn, *To Judge With Justice: History and Politics of Illinois Judicial Reform* (Urbana: University of Illinois Press, 1973), p. 105.

voting at the election, as required by the constitution. However, if any group's dissatisfaction with the main package could not be chanced in these final moments before *sine die* adjournment, it would be dissatisfaction on the part of the Chicago Democratic organization. Yet, the Democrats had just seen most-favored positions (the inclusion of multi-member districts with cumulative voting and election of judges in the main document) erode and ultimately vanish completely through a last ditch effort by a coalition of Republicans, independents and independent Democrats. Chicago Democrats had lost a battle and it would be some months before they could determine a strategy that would win the war.

The ballot, as it was finally presented to the voters, is shown in Figure 1.

THE ELECTION DATE

With the structure of the ballot now settled, the date for the referendum remained to be decided. The timing of the election could affect the outcome of the vote. The only 1870 constitutional constraint was that the election could not be less than two months nor more than six months after the adjournment of the convention.

Four time periods had been considered: a date before the general election on November 3, 1970; at the general election; soon after the November election; and at the beginning of the New Year. As the proceedings of the convention carried over into late summer, a pre-election referendum became unfeasible because of the two-month requirement of the 1870 constitution; it almost ruled out the general election as a viable option as well.

The new year had its supporters. Convention Vice-President John Alexander wanted the referendum set after the first of the year in hopes that eighteen-year-olds would have been nationally enfranchised. Convention President Witwer preferred a late November or early December date. Although not publicly articulated, the expectation was that the number of voters in a referendum at this time would be relatively small; especially so, after a major election. Furthermore, the major holidays would surely distract citizen attention from this momentous decision. In short, the electoral climate measured in terms of potential voter arousal was "cool." After carefully considering all of the options, the delegates finally selected December 15, 1970, as the referendum date.

FIGURE I.

OFFICIAL BALLOT

(Instructions to Voters: Place an "X" in the boxes opposite the propostitions for which you desire to vote. The full text of the proposed 1970 Constitution and the separate propositions is available for inspection in your voting unit.)

| Do you favor the proposed 1970 Constitution? | Yes |
| | No |

WHICH OF THE FOLLOWING PROVISIONS SHALL THE LEGISLATIVE ARTICLE OF THE PROPOSED 1970 CONSTITUTION CONTAIN CONCERNING THE ELECTION OF REPRESENTATIVES TO THE GENERAL ASSEMBLY? (Vote ONLY for one)

| Election of the 177 members of the House of Representatives from *multi-member districts by cumulative voting.* | 1A |

OR

| Election of the 177 members of the House of Representatives from *single member districts.* | 1B |

WHICH OF THE FOLLOWING PROVISIONS SHALL THE JUDICIAL ARTICLE OF THE PROPOSED 1970 CONSTITUTION CONTAIN CONCERNING THE SELECTION OF SUPREME, APPELLATE AND CIRCUIT COURT JUDGES? (Vote ONLY for one)

| The *election* by the voters of Judges nominated in primary elections or by petition. | 2A |

OR

| The *appointment* of Judges by the Governor from nominees submitted by Judicial Nominating Commissions. | 2B |

SHALL THE 1970 CONSTITUTION CONTAIN PROVISIONS:

| Abolishing the death penalty? | Yes |
| | No |

| Lowering the voting age to 18? | Yes |
| | No |

Source: Sixth Illinois Constitutional Convention, *Records of Proceedings,* vol. 1, p. 828.

VII

Campaign for the "Main Package"

We jumped onto a moving horse.

William Allen

Unlike the earlier campaign for a constitutional convention, the campaign for public acceptance of the proposed document was an isolated electoral event at which the only ballot considerations were the constitution and four separately submitted items. The new constitution had only to win approval of a simple majority of voters participating at this election. In other words, the special election would attract only voters interested in and/or informed about the issues at hand. The ratification campaign, therefore, demanded altogether different strategy decisions. The campaign for ratification also differed in style from the convention call campaign in that specific issues were publicly aired. This feature, combined with a contracted audience—the so-called attentive public—permitted a degree of sophistication lacking in 1968.

Among early endorsees of the proposed constitution was Governor Richard Ogilvie:

> The proposed 1970 Illinois constitution deserves the support of the people of Illinois. I urge everyone to join in a nonpartisan campaign to assure its ratification. For my own part, I will offer my assistance in organizing a citizen's committee to achieve that end. I am hopeful that leaders from all walks of life all over Illinois will join in this historic crusade.[1]

Neither the campaign committee, Illinois Citizens for a New Constitution (ICNC), nor their efforts toward adoption of the proposed constitution, was by the usual criteria, a "citizens' crusade." This

[1] *Illinois News*, September 16, 1970.

71

was partially the result of circumstance and partially an outcome of design. The ICNC itself comprised roughly fifty individuals representing endorsing organizations. Public relations director of the Illinois Agricultural Association, William Allen, served as campaign manager as he had done for the 1968 convention call campaign. The full committee met only once, while the executive committee met five times. The campaign group was able to function in this manner because relations established for the convention call campaign were sustained.

The Principal Actors and Their Campaign Strategy

In its campaign effort, the ICNC stressed a number of ideals that early survey data had shown were positively associated in the voters' minds with the new constitution. The campaigners suggested that the new document would (a) encourage pollution control, (b) enhance social justice, and (c) expand needed powers of local government.[2] Opponents too, however, could make specific claims about the proposed constitution—such as the consolidation of counties and the elimination of county offices—that raised fears in some voters' minds. It was difficult to counter such arguments.

Nor could the campaign for adoption of a new constitution directly confront the 1870 constitution. Strategists had initially planned such a campaign—a "vote the rascals out" policy—but survey data indicated that this was not an advisable tactic.[3] This had also been found to be true during the 1968 convention call campaign. Most voters were not prepared to accept their current constitution as useless. Rather, they preferred an argument that the constitutional convention had reviewed the old constitution, kept those provisions intact that were still serviceable, and revised those that needed improvement or modernization. In other words, a low-key not an aggressive campaign seemed called for.

Another reason for following a limited campaign strategy was that the October survey indicated a stratum of preexisting support for the proposed constitution. In fact, it was felt that exposure to the campaign and its issues would have a negative affect upon these voters. This had not been true during the convention campaign, when surveys in the summer of 1968 indicated support among

---

[2] ICNC New Campaign Strategy, mimeo, undated.

[3] Leo T. Shapiro and Associates, Inc., *Pre-Ratification Election Survey* (Chicago, Illinois, October 1970). Sample Size: 443

informed voters and increasing support as increased information became available. Now, however, as the 1970 campaign progressed, the proportion of survey respondents who said they would vote for the new constitution dropped sharply.

TABLE I. SUPPORT FOR PROPOSED CONSTITUTION[4]

	Mid-October	End November (Call Back)
For	55%	40%
Against	18	13
Undecided	27	47
(N = 443)	100	100

Between the October and November survey periods the first set of campaign materials had been sent out by campaign headquarters and all registered voters in Illinois had received a copy of the proposed constitution together with explanations of the document. The secretary of state had published 12 million copies, of which approximately 5.5 million copies, with explanatory text, were mailed to the electorate and 4.5 million appeared as newspaper inserts. Some 700,000 copies were placed in weekly papers and the remainder were kept for special requests. This outpouring of information impressed at least some conscientious voters who felt obliged to take another look at the issues before making their decision.

A third reason for deciding to maintain a low campaign profile, was the belief that undecided voters, if activated, would not support the constitution. This was later borne out by postelection survey data indicating that a majority of negative voters had been undecided only weeks before the election, whereas most "yes" voters had decided to support the proposed document even before the campaign for ratification.[5]

Campaign strategists developed a list of "target areas" throughout the state which had demonstrated significant support for earlier constitutional reform elections. Specifically, major concentrations of voters were evaluated in terms of their relative turnout for the convention call in 1968. From these tallies the 1970 "yes" vote potential was developed. Based on this information, the Chicago metropolitan area became a prime campaign target (71 percent of

[4]*Pre-Ratification Election Survey.*
[5]Geomedia, *Constitution Post-Election Study* (Chicago, Illinois, January 1971). Sample Size: 482

the "yes" votes were calculated to lie within fifty miles of "the loop"), as were the Peoria, Champaign, and Carbondale areas; at the same time, East St. Louis, the largest downstate population center, was almost totally disregarded by the committee because it had so strongly opposed the convention call.

Finally, campaign strategy was affected by both time and limited money. Organizers had roughly three months to put together a campaign, which by itself curtailed any possibility of a comprehensive electoral strategy. Instead, workers utilized the "rifle" technique, with the greatest stress applied directly at points guaranteed to produce the greatest reward. Pressed for time, those who had led the successful 1968 campaign for the convention call met prior to adjournment of the convention to lay organizational groundwork and map a basic campaign plan.[6] However, lack of time was not as great a handicap as it might have seemed. In 1968, organizers had had to start at the beginning, but now a momentum already existed: those who had served in various capacities in 1968 were willing to resume their tasks; organizations were endorsing the proposed constitution without solicitation; and many people were already aware of the impending election. "We jumped onto a moving horse," campaign manager Allen said aptly.[7] As supporters became increasingly aware, a short campaign actually proved to be of greater benefit than harm to the constitutional cause. As time elapsed, voter interest waned and the opposition gained strength.

The lack of sufficient financing acted as the greatest single deterrent to any notions of a saturation campaign, especially since funds were misallocated because contributions turned out to be much lower than anticipated. Three budgets —"mini," "midi," and "maxi"— were developed prior to the initial fund-raising. The mini budget of $243,660 was declared unacceptable by the campaign manager.[8] However, solicitations ultimately brought in only $167,000—far short of even the "unacceptable" mini budget. "By the time we realized that contributions were not coming in a manner we had hoped, it was too late to shift budgeted appropriations."[9] The heaviest single cutback was in newspaper advertising, although this had been in past elections the major source of blue ballot information for voters. The electronic media campaign had to be planned and put

[6]Presentation by William Allen to the Public Relations Society of America, p. 4 (undated).
[7]Interview with William Allen, December 15, 1970.
[8]Interview with William Allen, April 28, 1971.
[9]Ibid.

together before the financial situation was fully realized, and consequently siphoned off a disproportionate amount of available resources. "Free" newspaper advertising was then sought by the committee in the form of news-making events such as a planned demonstration for the new constitution at the Civic Center in Chicago and a flying whistle-stop tour in six Illinois cities on the Monday before the election by members of a number of organizations representing labor, agricultural, educational, business and church groups. On the same Monday, Illinois Education Association President W. Dwight Knows also conducted an eleven-hour flying tour to Illinois cities to encourage teachers to support the constitution. Moreover, much of the press was favorably disposed to the new constitution and ran editorials to that effect. Some 250 daily and weekly newspapers also carried the official explanation of the constitution as a supplement to their regular edition.

Despite the financial setback, the realization that there already existed basic support for the new constitution, and that voters felt a good deal of loyalty for the existing constitution so that an aggressive campaign did not seem in order, there were inevitably those who hoped for more activity. Some proponents may have become genuinely concerned that their hopes for a new constitution would be dashed by inactivity especially as they watched the opposition become increasingly vocal. One such group called itself Save Our State (SOS); it was especially strong in suburban Chicago, Peoria, Champaign, and Bloomington and was active as far south as Carbondale. Without any apparent centralized campaign for adoption of the constitution, the opposition would have appeared greater than the actual numbers warranted. The citizens' committee offset the potential for distortion of the size of the opposition, although not in terms of "overkill." "Our campaign," explained Alllen, "did not affect the win for the new constitution but did keep it from failing." [10] Overall credit for the victory must be given to the endorsement by the Cook County Democratic party and the active campaigning by convention delegates in their home districts. Without either, the campaign for ratification would have been seriously jeopardized, if not totally lost.

Tactics by the Democratic organization to delay endorsement of the constitution provided the only sense of excitement (although not appreciated) in an otherwise calm campaign atmosphere. A collective sigh of relief by supporters of the constitution accompanied

[10]Interview with William Allen, April 26, 1971.

the formal endorsement by Chicago Mayor Richard J. Daley, chairman of the Cook County Democratic party, on November 30, just two weeks prior to the election. The Democratic endorsement was cited by campaign manager Allen as the single most important event of the three-month campaign. The effect of Daley's endorsement upon voter opinions is clearly evidenced by shifts in survey results following the announcement.

TABLE II. EFFECT OF DALEY ENDORSEMENT[11]

Proposed Constitution	Monday Survey November 30	Tuesday Survey December 1	Overnight Shift
For	40%	49%	+ 9%
Against	13	15	+ 2
Undecided	47	36	− 11
(N = 443)	100	100	

The overnight rise in support by voters for the proposed constitution can only be attributed to the Democratic party blessing. However, surveys of voter intentions never again reached the early October figure of 55 percent in favor, which was close to the percentage of affirmative votes actually cast at the election.

Even if the overall ICNC campaign seemed low-key to some, individual delegates were anything but. Roughly 100 delegates actively campaigned for adoption of the proposed constitution throughout the state and frequently in areas untouched by the Chicago-based committee. The effect of this activity would be evident in numerous instances. For example, two counties voted for the constitution and broke long-standing traditions in doing so. It was only the second time since 1950 that Edwards and Wabash counties had approved any sort of constitutional change. Further, Edwards County voted two to one for the constitution, a ratio of support equaled by only two other counties in the state (Morgan and Cook). One of the major factors in the turnaround for these counties along the Wabash River had to have been the promotional efforts of convention delegate Henry Hendren in Edwards County.[12] Delegate enthusiasm and the desire to complete what had been begun nine months earlier, carried these campaigns through three months of intensive activity. Responses by sixty-nine delegates to a mailed

[11]*Pre-Ratification Election Survey.*
[12]*Chicago Sun-Times,* December 20, 1970.

questionnaire concerning their campaign activities indicated that each made an average of six public appearances per week. Voters surveyed after the election listed delegates as their second major source of information during the campaign (the primary source being newspapers). Moreover, contact with delegates induced more affirmative than negative voting on the constitution. Apparently delegates had earlier developed a reservoir of public respect. Voters surveyed at the conclusion of the convention overwhelmingly claimed that delegates were well qualified and took their jobs seriously.[13]

Delegates typically spoke before groups in their own districts or communities. Occasionally, they teamed up to accommodate wider geographical areas. For example, one team of six delegates from southern Illinois barnstormed the twenty-eight counties of their three districts, appearing together one night each week in a different location.[14] It was more common, however, for delegates in the Chicago area to campaign together. Attempts by some delegates to organize formally into collective campaign efforts, such as the delegate speakers bureaus used by the Maryland and Hawaiian constitutional conventions or the "task forces" organized by Connecticut delegates, met with little enthusiasm, since most delegates preferred to set their own pace and style.

The most serious obstacle to ratification was the manner and degree in which opponents to the proposed document capitalized upon the revenue issue. The possibility of a taxpayers' revolt manifesting itself as constitutional negativism undercut the optimism concerning public acceptance of the proposed constitution. Early in the campaign, constitutional proponent Alan J. Dixon (Illinois state treasurer) proclaimed darkly, "I weep for the chances of passing. . . . I've never seen the electorate as tax conscious as they are now. I can't conceive of the voters giving unlimited taxing powers to the legislature."[15] Only one week before the referendum, State Attorney General William Scott added his own doubts, saying that the constitution was in trouble because voters with whom he had spoken expressed confusion and reservations about the revenue article.[16]

According to Andrew Hacker of Cornell University, overhauled constitutions are widely viewed as free-wheeling documents:

[13] *Pre-Ratification Election Survey.*
[14] *Champaign-Urbana Courier*, November 9, 1970.
[15] *Chicago Daily News*, September 17, 1970.
[16] *Illinois State Register*, December 8, 1970.

"Voting them down is part of a new style populism in the U.S. which is also manifesting itself in the growing number of school bond issues which are being defeated . . . it is really a vote against authority."[17]

Undercurrents of dissent, stimulated principally by the revenue issue, were also felt by the constitutional campaign committee. Campaign Director Allen estimated a $200,000 loss in contributions from business because of serious doubts by some businessmen concerning local taxation. The Civic Federation of Chicago did not endorse the constitution. Allen said, "If the State Chamber of Commerce had not endorsed, we would have had a full-scale business revolt on our hands."[18] The campaign committee was understandably concerned; given the amount of opposition that had surfaced because of the revenue issue, they assumed that there existed a latent reservoir of discontent which would flow forth only on election day.

Into this reservoir of discontent dipped the opposition. With few exceptions, they stressed revenue matters. Their specific effectiveness cannot be measured, but the campaign committee for the constitution felt threatened enough to highlight tax benefits in their campaign literature despite directives by survey data to *avoid revenue issues*. The four items being submitted to the voters as separate issues were treated as the controversial items. Thus the opposition, if the potential voter negativism was to become an electoral reality, had to create a controversy out of the revenue issue and drag it out into the open. However, they never succeeded in doing so.

The revenue article never became a major issue for one principal reason: the Illinois state legislature, in the summer of 1969, enacted a state income tax. Had this move been left for the new constitution, both would surely have been defeated. In a survey conducted months prior to the constitutional convention and just before passage of the income tax, respondents by a two-to-one margin indicated their belief that a new constitution should not allow an income tax.[19] Opponents of the constitution would have possessed a clear target, the tax itself, to motivate the tax-conscious electorate. In effect, passage of the income tax under the provisions of the 1870 constitution served ideally the proponents of the new constitution,

---

[17]*Wall Street Journal*, December 15, 1970.

[18]*Interview* with William Allen, April 28, 1971; a similar comment was made by Samuel Witwer, in an interview on January 16, 1971.

[19]University of Illinois Survey Research Laboratory, *Mini-Omnibus Study #043* (Urbana, Illinois, spring 1969). Sample Size: 603

permitting them to argue that the proposed constitution placed restrictions upon the tax which did not exist under the old charter.[20]

OTHER ACTORS IN THE CAMPAIGN

With the conspicuous exception of the Civic Federation of Chicago, organizations which had endorsed the convention call in 1968 similarly endorsed the proposed constitution. As in the 1968 campaign, these organizations sought principally to inform their own memberships rather than develop any overall campaign strategy. The only formal link many of these groups had with one another, therefore, was the citizens' campaign headquarters.

One factor complicating any effort to centralize activities among the endorsing groups, was the strong differences they had on the issues being submitted separately from the main document. For example, the State Chamber of Commerce supported retention of multi-member legislative districts, while the Chicago Association of Commerce and Industry endorsed single-member districts. The Chicago Bar Association favored multi-member districts and the League of Women Voters preferred single-member districts. Some large organizations refrained from endorsing the separate issues altogether. Yet all of these groups strongly supported the main document.

The organizations which did not assume positions on the side issues had fairly heterogeneous memberships that were difficult to mobilize. These groups included the major educational associations, the Illinois Educational Association and the Illinois Congress of Parents and Teachers as well as the Illinois Municipal League, which spans the full spectrum of cities and villages within the state. The relatively homogeneous groups like the Chicago Bar Association and the Illinois Agricultural Association were in a better position to evaluate and recommend alternatives suited to their specialized interests.

All major organizations that supported the main document pursued a policy of selective endorsement in which the constitution

---

[20]Thus, proponents could argue in their campaign literature, "Vote yes for the 1970 Illinois Constitution to: prohibit specifically a graduated state income tax—no limits in the present constitution." From "Vote Yes for the 1970 Constitution," undated pamphlet, Citizens' Committee for a New Constitution.

was "good" or "better" than its century-old counterpart because of specific sections or articles within its framework. Attention was therefore drawn to points directly related to the functions and purposes of the special interest associations. For example, business groups stressed portions of the new revenue article although the Small Businessmen's Association was opposed to the new constitution because of the antidiscrimination in hiring clauses in the Bill of Rights and because citizen's pollution suits were guaranteed by the environmental article. Education groups naturally advertised the provisions of an improved education article as well as the revenue article. The Illinois Municipal League and the Illinois Commission on Urban Area Government (appointed by the governor) stressed the strengths of the new local government article, specifically the provisions on municipal home rule and intergovernmental relations. The degree to which groups were able to support the entire constitution on the basis of a cherished specific portion is demonstrated in the formal statement of endorsement by the Commission on Urban Area Government:

> In conformance with the desires of the majority of its membership, the Commission endorses the main package of the proposed new constitution *as a necessary condition* to the adoption of the local government article. (Emphasis added).[21]

Contrary to the policy of the citizens' committee to avoid a comparison between the proposed constitution and some model state constitution, which would naturally cast shadows upon the merits of the document, few groups refrained from a discussion of the "Phantom Third Constitution." Most organizations that appealed to their memberships prefaced their arguments with "the proposed constitution is not the best we could have written but it is better than the 1870 constitution and therefore worthy of your support because . . ." While the ad hoc nature of the citizens' campaign committee enabled it to avoid mentioning this "phantom third," permanent organizations could not indulge in such strategic side-stepping. These groups have long-standing policy positions and members had to be made aware of the fact that the constitution was a product of compromises that did not always result in inclusion of some favored positions. A simple means had to be found to justify the endorsement of a constitution that did not compare ideally to all of each group's policies.

[21] *Illinois News*, November 23, 1970.

Arguments by groups opposed to the constitution reflected both ends of the political spectrum, although the principal target for attack was usually the same—the revenue article. This did not come as a surprise to the citizens' campaign committee and other proponents of the constitution. To the right, local SOS committees assumed a variety of forms, including one group, which attempted to synchronize the activities of all the others, called the Coordinating Committee to Defeat the Proposed Constitution. The distribution of approximately one million SOS pamphlets stressed what these groups believed to be guarantees for "confiscatory taxation, unlimited spending and metropolitan regional government." [22] These claims did not so much win converts as they reinforced preexisting fears. It is, however, difficult to assess realistically the effect of these SOS groups on voter behavior in this election. Although SOS speakers bureaus were flooded with requests throughout the campaign,[23] this was not a particularly accurate measure of opposition to the constitution. Many requests reflected only a desire by soliciting groups to present a balanced picture of the proposed constitution. Nonetheless, these engagements gave the opposition an opportunity to be heard.

On the political left, those groups opposed to the constitution, specifically labor organizations, made little attempt to reach voters beyond their own memberships. In fact, opposition by labor was, at best, token. Their only real effort was a series of editorials in the state AFL-CIO newsletter and distribution at meetings of some 500,000 pamphlets. Active compaigning by COPE (the political arm of the AFL-CIO) was limited almost exclusively to the East St. Louis area. Maneuverings by the Chicago Federation of Labor were constrained by the Cook County Democratic party endorsement. Opposition by labor was further weakened by the endorsement of the proposed constitution by the United Auto Workers (UAW). However, the UAW stood with the AFL-CIO in opposition to single-member legislative districts and selection of the judiciary by appointment, although Robert Johnson, director of UAW Region 4, had supported the merit plan for selecting judges during committee deliberations at the convention.[24]

On the whole, the AFL-CIO publicly opposed the revenue article (specifically, the restriction on a graduated income tax, the eight-

[22]Save Our State Committee, "Know the Truth About the Proposed Constitution (Winnetka, undated pamphlet).
[23]*Beacon News*, Aurora, November 30, 1970.
[24]Press Release of the UAW, July 8, 1970.

to-five corporate-to-individual tax ratio, and the absence of an income tax limit) and the manner in which the constitution was presented to the voters. Yet, arguments along this line were contradictory. On the one hand, the AFL-CIO wanted a piece-by-piece adoption of the constitution,[25] but on the other, it complained that a major failure of the constitutional convention was the exclusion of certain issues as separate electoral questions. What labor really wanted was the submission of the revenue article as a separate issue, but the inclusion in the main document of the plan for multi-member legislative districts with cumulative voting.[26]

Another major group to oppose the new constitution, and for similar reasons, was the Illinois State Conference of the NAACP. The NAACP stressed tax inequities in the main document and opposed both single-member districts ("cumulative voting helps blacks have representation in the state legislature") and judicial appointment ("in most cases, blacks are overlooked in appointment").[27] However, as in the case of labor, there was internal disagreement. Thus Operation Breadbasket (of the Southern Christian Leadership Conference) supported the main package and especially merit selection of judges. In any case, NAACP opposition came late in the campaign and had little effect. Blacks for the most part were influenced in their voting by other factors, especially the Democratic party.

Altogether, the effect by both opposing and supporting organizations on their memberships was negligible. Despite the importance placed by the ICNC upon organizational endorsements and despite efforts by these groups to inform their members, few voters mentioned their group's position when surveyed weeks after the election. Specifically, of 240 instances of group membership reported by respondents, the great majority (210) did not know whether the organization in which they claimed membership had favored or opposed adoption of the new constitution.[28]

There was less confusion among voters about the positions of the major political parties, especially the Democratic party. Chicago Democrats did not immediately jump on the bandwagon. Delegate Paul Elward, one of Mayor Daley's chief spokesmen at the constitu-

[25]*Chicago Sun-Times*, November 11, 1970.

[26]*Chicago Sun-Times*, September 21, 1970.

[27]*Illinois State Journal*, December 9, 1970.

[28]Leo T. Shapiro and Associates, Inc., *Post-Election Survey* (Chicago, Illinois, January 1971). Sample Size: 443

tional convention, in the last hours of formal deliberation asserted, "It's a monstrosity, a first-class mess and I can't be anything but pessimistic about its chances for acceptance."[29] This attitude, coupled with the mayor's notable absence from the closing ceremonies of the convention, triggered very serious doubts about whether the document would gain sufficient votes. Moreover, campaign workers had to wait until the end of November for Daley's formal endorsement of the work of the convention. It was believed that Daley's boycott of the signing ceremonies was his means of expressing dissatisfaction with the last-minute defeat of the Democrats on the questions of legislative representation and judicial selection. When the coalition of Republicans and independents pushed through the plan to put these two issues entirely outside the main package, the Democrats were confronted with the question of how precinct captains could instruct Chicago voters on each ballot question. It was argued by some that, rather than risk voter confusion and possible approval of appointment of the judiciary, the Mayor would not support the constitution. Others believed that Daley would express lukewarm support for the main package but tell his ward committeemen to have precinct captains instruct voters to cast votes against it; however, it is highly unlikely that Daley would engage in such contrivances. Power over the Democratic organization in Chicago was measured in terms of publicly claimed intentions, and such a move would give the appearance that Daley was losing control of a vast electoral machine. Although it was possible that the Democratic organization would not endorse the constitution, the Mayor was well aware of a number of advantages for Chicago in the proposed constitution, including broad home rule powers, a constitutional basis for de facto classification of real property in Cook County, and a potential for public financial aid to the Chicago Board of Education.

In the last week of November, the Democratic party at last turned to consideration of the impending election at public hearings in Springfield and Chicago. The hearings had been provided for by the 1970 Democratic platform as the substitute for any formal position on the proposed constitution. The Republican Platform Committee had earlier endorsed the constitution. Generally, testimony in Springfield before the state committee, chaired by Elward, encouraged endorsement of the constitution. Witnesses were principally

---

[29]Informal interview with the author.

Democrats and represented a range of interests, including a number of college students extolling the virtues of the eighteen-year-old vote and members of the Illinois Association of Senior Citizens, urging support of the main document as a means of acquiring tax relief for the elderly through homestead exemptions which had recently been struck down as unconstitutional under the revenue provisions of the 1870 Constitution. In the testimony before the Democratic committee in Chicago, both Democrats and Republicans were split. At both hearing sites, Chairman Elward claimed that the purpose of these hearings was to acquaint the committee with popular sentiments for and against the constitution as an aid and guide to their decision on the matter.

In fact, few believed the function of these hearings was informational. Some believed they were a facade—an attempt to democratize what was likely to be an authoritarian decision on the fate of the proposed constitution. Was Daley looking for excuses amid extensive testimony to oppose the document? Yet more witnesses supported the document than opposed it. John Dreiske, in an editorial in the *Chicago Sun-Times,* suggested a plausible explanation:

> There are various reasons why the Democrats proved loath to carry the Con-Con issue into the November 3 election campaign, preferring to leave it for afterward, leading up to the December 15 referendum. . . . For instance, there are important voting blocs in opposition to the proposed new constitution. One is the state's AFL-CIO which, in the Peoria state convention, voted to reject the constitution. So the Democrats would prefer to enter the picture, probably in favor of the constitution, after November 3 when Con-Con will be on its own. This stratagem tends to save the Daley candidates from active opposition of those who don't like the new constitution.[30]

The close political relationship between the Democrats and labor is known. Many, therefore, viewed the formal opposition to the constitution by the Chicago Federation of Labor as a prelude to Daley's opposition.[31] Of course, Daley had defied labor's position on calling the constitutional convention in 1968. That he might defy labor again was not unthinkable—but caution was required. In order not to risk closely contested races in Cook County, specifically the presidency of the Cook County Board, and a distinct possibility of gaining a majority in the state House of Representatives, it was politically expedient at that time for Mayor Daley to avoid antagonizing his strongest electoral ally.

[30]John Dreiske, *Chicago Sun-Times,* October 7, 1970.
[31]Robert Hartley, *Metro-East Journal,* September 27, 1970.

For whatever reason, the hearings were a dramatic political gesture which turned media attention to the Democratic party and its cliff-hanging decision. The Daley endorsement subsequently received banner headlines in all major Chicago and many downstate newspapers. The overnight effect on voter intentions regarding the proposed constitution was a 9 percent overall shift from the undecided to the affirmative column.

There is no doubt that the Democratic organization was responsible for the relatively high turnout in Chicago. This was especially significant because the constitutional issue would not be expected to interest precinct captains and "spur them to their most enthusiastic doorbell ringing."[32] However, a *Chicago Tribune* survey of Democratic ward committeemen after Daley's announcement of support for the constitution two weeks prior to the referendum, did indicate that party regulars intended to back up the Mayor's endorsement with work at the precinct level.[33] A Westside committeeman, who said he personally opposed the proposed document, nevertheless claimed he would make the effort in his area because he was a "team player." Two "team players" did not participate in the campaign for ratification, and theirs were the only wards in the city (25th and 32nd) to vote against the constitution. This fact in no way represented a loosening of the Mayor's organization. Rather, it was indicative of the effect the Democratic "machine" could have upon voters at a time when voters were otherwise indifferent. In these particular wards, leaders chose not to exert their influence. In the 25th ward, Alderman Vito Marzullo confessed, "We left everything to their [the voters] judgment. We didn't distribute any sample ballots. . . . we just kept away from it."[34] Not only did the constitution lose in the 25th by almost a two-to-one margin, but turnout was exceedingly low—23.8 percent as compared, for example, to 57.7 percent in Mayor Daley's own ward. At a press conference the day after the election, Daley announced, "I am proud of the part the Democratic party played in this."

The role of the governor in the campaign was less conspicuous, and few of his speeches on the constitution reached a broad audience. His attempts to influence the Republican party throughout the state were necessarily soft-pedaled. In the final days of the campaign a telegram sent by Ogilvie to all 102 Illinois Republican

---

[32]Dreiske, *Chicago Sun-Times*, December 16, 1970.
[33]*Chicago Tribune*, December 2, 1970.
[34]*Chicago Sun-Times*, December 20, 1970.

county chairmen reminded them of the 1970 Republican platform endorsement of the constitution. "I urge you and your organization to devote full energies to procuring the greatest possible affirmative vote in your county on Tuesday. I will be grateful for your support in this vital matter."[35] It is not surprising that greater numbers of voters surveyed after the election were aware of Mayor Daley's position on the constitution than of Governor Ogilvie's.

[35]*Illinois News*, December 11, 1970.

VIII

The Mini-Campaigns

"2-B or Not 2-B" . . . and other questions.
Judicial reform campaign slogan

The technique of submitting certain sections of a revised constitution to the voters as separate issues, to be voted on apart from the main package, is popularly considered the best means of dealing with controversial issues at the polls. According to this view, then, the four separate questions of the 1970 constitutional referendum in Illinois were the controversial issues. However, the main document proposed a number of potentially more controversial items—measured in terms of departure from preexisting practices—than is initially apparent. Some argued that the four propositions submitted separately to the voters were merely smokescreens intended to distract voters from seeing certain portions of the bill of rights and the revenue and local government articles. In this view the separate submissions, in effect, took the heat off the main body of the constitution and sections in it that were at least as controversial, electorally speaking, as the four so-called sacrificial lambs. A case in point was the attempt to offer a proposition to the voters regarding an upper limit on the income tax. The attempt failed on the floor of the convention by one vote. Proponents of an unlimited income tax conceded the unpopularity of this position electorally but resisted the special treatment of the question arguing that this would undoubtedly drag the remainder of the revenue article into the glare of the campaign. Opponents of the view that the separate submissions were a mere smokescreen pointed out, with some justification, that without the options for selecting legislative and judicial officials, no structural changes would have been offered the public and for that reason alone these questions were *the crucial issues* of the 1970 constitutional referendum.

The Illinois Citizens for a New Constitution (ICNC) decided to avoid the separate constitutional issues in hopes of gaining wide organizational support for the main document. Support of the constitution by both major political parties was considered crucial. Precisely on the issues of legislative representation and judicial selection, however, bipartisan support had broken down. There was no alternative, therefore, to separate campaigns on these questions. Visible campaigns were developed on the issues of legislative representation, judicial selection, and abolition of the death penalty. On the eighteen-year-old vote issue, campaigning was less systematic. In order to maximize support in each case, the campaigns maintained no official relations with one another and were, for all practical purposes, isolated efforts. Delegates, however, largely ignored this strategem with many of them airing their personal views on all or most of the separate submissions.

LEGISLATIVE REPRESENTATION (SEPARATE QUESTION No. 1)

The campaign to change the method of electing members to the Illinois House of Representatives, i.e. in favor of single-member districts (ballot option 1-B) was shaped almost exclusively by the availability of manpower, financial limitations, and a perceived need to dig in against the Democratic organization in Chicago, which favored the continuation of cumulative voting in multi-member districts (ballot option 1-A). A proposed budget of $17,000 eventually had to be reduced to $9,200, with downstate contributions accounting for 70 percent of that total. Campaign Director William Sommerschield (a convention delegate who had served on the Legislative Committee) proposed that the major portion of resources be expended "where it counted: in the marketplace." Therefore, only 14 percent of available resources was allocated to office management and 86 percent to advertising. This meant that formal campaign headquarters never materialized. The part-time campaign officers and staff consisted of "blue ribbon" delegates (political reformers), diehard convention staff who had sought the demise of multi-member districts in committee and floor deliberations and were now determined to take the issue to the people, and would-be legislators who sought to enhance their own electoral prospects.

The Citizens for Single-Member Districts mounted campaigns to increase awareness of the issue and to educate the public on its importance. A lack of finances severely limited the former and time, the latter. A nationally respected advertising firm assisted in putting together a program. The educational program included information on the abuses of the multi-member district/cumulative voting system (proposition 1-A) which the committee contended would be corrected by single-member districts; this information was distributed to major newspapers (the Lindsay-Schaub newspaper chain endorsed proposition 1-B), as well as television and radio outlets. In addition, a seventeen-page comprehensive pamphlet entitled "Option 1-B, the Merits of Single-Member Legislative Districts" was sent to county, community, and other local party leaders in the hope of educating these influential persons on the question of legislative representation in the state of Illinois. Approximately 18,000 copies of the booklet were distributed in this fashion. A set of five lecture-sized charts depicting graphically the abuses of cumulative voting were also sent to delegates, speakers bureaus, and local groups. The educational campaign was designed to pin down the specific problems of the cumulative voting formula, implying and often stating that these conditions would be eliminated by adopting the legislative alternative. Proposition 1-B was offered as an "improvement" rather than a "reform." This was calculated to intercept downstate negativism to constitutional change.

Unlike the educational campaign, the awareness campaign simply promoted proposition 1-B and did not attempt to explain or defend it. As part of this effort, 1-B proponents secured a number of highway billboards throughout the major metropolitan areas of the state (although boards were not available in some communities). The large boards, in deep blue with white lettering, said only, "Vote Option 1-B." It was believed that when an electoral issue is complex a simple trigger phrase such as this is usually effective. Approximately 50,000 flyers were also distributed in the final days before the election at railroad stations, subways, and entrances to underground garages in Chicago. This was the only attempt by the campaign committee to reach suburban Chicago voters. The media campaign was most severely restricted by the lack of funds. Television and radio advertising had to be abandoned entirely. However, "free" advertising was sought by the committee at press conferences in Chicago and Springfield a week before the election.

Little formal organization developed to maintain cumulative voting (proposition 1-A) except for scattered activity by a number of legislators who, rightly or wrongly, questioned their own futures under the new system. Opposition to legislative reform was especially strong in the Chicago metropolitan area (specifically, the counties of Cook, Lake, DuPage, and Will). All four major Chicago dailies editorially supported cumulative voting. Yet, none of this generalized sentiment jelled into a structured campaign effort. Even the Cook County Democratic party, which provided vigorous opposition to judicial appointment, was not particularly active in its opposition to single-member districts. It is uncertain whether this was because legislative selection was not as important to Cook County Democrats as many believed or because they perceived little campaign opposition to proposition 1–A in the Chicago area. The latter seems more likely.

Supporters of legislative reform had few illusions that their issue would succeed at the special election. A notice to the steering committee of Citizens for Single-Member Districts, just one week before the election, read in part:

> On to Victory, December 15th! But, if victory does not come to 1B, several courses of action are available for the future: a test of the constitutionality of multi-member districts and cumulative voting; work in General Assembly for constitutional amendment to provide single-member districts and (assuming the new Constitution passes) an initiative referendum campaign.

Yet, 39 percent of voters throughout the state supported proposition 1–B. In fact single-member districts actually carried in over two-thirds of Illinois counties, notably (and ironically) in areas where information from the committee about proposition 1–B had not permeated. This downstate vote was not large enough, however, to overcome the strong Cook County support (59 percent) for retaining cumulative voting. As it turned out, most support for 1–B predated the vigorous downstate effort. In October, 46 percent of respondents to a statewide survey claimed they would vote for 1–B if the election were "held today."[1] It should also be noted that confusion about the legislative issue may have induced fluke victories for 1–B in many areas since: (a) 15 percent of respondents to a survey just three weeks after the election did not remember how they had voted on the issue (compared to only 2 percent who did not remember how they had voted on the judicial question); and (b) interviewers in a postelection survey noted confused responses by voters, such as, "I think I voted for the type of districts we have always had—single-member districts."

[1] Leo T. Shapiro and Associates, Inc., *Pre-Ratification Election Survey* (Chicago, Illinois, October 1970). Sample Size: 443

Judicial Selection (Separate Question No. 2)

It was a political format that styled the campaign for proposition 2–B calling for the merit appointment of judges. By adopting party ground rules, and particularly precinct organization in at least the Chicago metropolitan area, (and to which most of the committee's efforts were in fact limited) the Citizens Committee for Better Courts confronted major party opposition to this judicial reform on its own terms. No previous constitutional amendment campaign in Illinois attempted to employ this type of comprehensive strategy, nor did the citizens' campaigns for the main document or for other separate issues at this election do so.

The campaign for proposition 2–B did not suffer for lack of financing or manpower. Unlike the campaign for option 1–B in favor of single-member legislative districts, the 2–B campaign with a budget of $170,000 (exceeding even the budget of the ICNC), managed to show a number of thirty-second television spots throughout the state. In addition, campaign organizers had a pool of volunteers, primarily members of the Chicago Bar, to turn to at various stages of the campaign. Whereas only five organizations endorsed the concept of single-member districts, more than twenty national, state and local organizations, representing business, agricultural, civic, women's, religious, educational, and professional groups, endorsed proposition 2–B. All of this was supplemented by strong editorial support in the Chicago metropolitan area.

The campaign for 2–B had other advantages as well, including an organizational foundation and numerous individuals who had geared up for this effort for almost twenty years, a period that had included two judicial amendment campaigns (1958 and 1962) and that had culminated in an active lobbying role, as the Committee for Modern Courts, at the constitutional convention. The dedication of those committed to judicial reform is best exemplified by one of this campaign's most active workers, Wayne W. Whalen, a delegate who served on the Judiciary Committee and as chairman of the Committee on Style, Drafting and Submission. According to Rubin Cohn, staff counsel to the Judiciary Committee, Whalen "came to the convention totally and unreservedly committed to the merit plan."[2]

Formal offices for a campaign organization, the Committee for Better Courts in Illinois, opened in October in both Chicago and

[2]Rubin G. Cohn, *To Judge With Justice: History and Politics of Illinois Judicial Reform* (Urbana: University of Illinois Press, 1973), p. 46.

Springfield. A functional breakdown of campaign duties followed closely the pattern of the 1967 campaign organization for merit selection in Colorado.[3] There were, for example, individuals responsible for finances, public relations, local committees, a speakers bureau, and political mobilization.

A basic lesson of the Colorado experience had been that lawyers should not be in the forefront of a campaign to amend the judicial selection process—the tag of "lawyers' amendment" is the kiss of death, electorally. Hence, the rule is to set up a campaign of non-lawyers displaying campaign workers and supporters with a wide range of interests. The avoidance of the lawyer stigma was a persistent campaign direction. The best illustration of this effort was the television advertisement aired statewide in the last week before the election. Flashed in sequence were representatives (typically dressed) of all major walks of life: farmer, laborer, policeman, housewife, businessman, and so forth. A further reflection of the policy of avoidance was the creation of an independent committee of lawyers in favor of merit selection: Lawyers for 2–B. The committee was comprised jointly of members of the Illinois State Bar Association and the Chicago Bar Association. Their slogan was simply "2–B or not 2–B." Their major objective in the overall campaign was to dissolve the claim of professional domination of the campaign for merit appointment. It should be noted, however, that the legal profession in the state of Illinois was by no means entirely in favor of merit selection. Downstate lawyers, often representatives of county or city bar associations, waged vigorous opposition campaigns in their areas. In fact, Springfield, the downstate headquarters for the Committee for Better Courts, was at the same time a particularly negative region. Opposition rested principally upon the belief that the Chicago Bar Association would inevitably dominate the proposed selection process.

The Colorado experience also provided advocates of merit selection with a vocabulary of campaign terms to avoid or to stress. Such words as "commissions," "governor," and "appointment" produced an undesirable reaction among a majority of voters. On the other hand, such terms as "selection" and "merit" were positive. In addition, a number of state referendum campaigns for merit selection of judges reinforced the basic theme, "keep our judges out of politics." Advocates of proposition 2–B consequently adapted this theme for

---

[3] Alvred Heinicke, "The Colorado Amendment Story," *Judicature* 51 (1967): 226.

their own materials and media campaign: "Vote politics out of our courts."

Distribution of materials was extensive. Roughly 2.5 million brochures were distributed throughout the state, in addition to 500,000 election day cards to all known sympathetic voters in the Chicago area. A limited edition of Spanish brochures was also dispensed to the Spanish-speaking community in Chicago and to producers of Spanish-language radio programs. The campaign committee purchased a number of thirty-second television spots, forty in Chicago and thirty downstate, to be aired in the last two weeks before the election. The film was produced by the public relations firm of the committee and emphasized a diffused "voice of the people" whose concern and outrage over the present practice of electing judges was apparent.

The media campaign favoring merit selection also used endorsements by a number of well-known individuals, including U.S. Senator Adlai Stevenson III and Governor Richard B. Ogilvie. National figures such as Warren Burger, chief justice of the U.S. Supreme Court, former Justice Arthur Goldberg, and Ronald Reagan, governor of California, also endorsed the plan.

On balance, however, traditional political party tactics were the most effective tools in the campaign for merit selection. The key was a coalition of preexisting components of election organizations, specifically a reactivation of the Stevenson precinct organization in the suburbs and the city-wide organization of the Independent Voters of Illinois. The political mobilization section of the campaign organization concentrated on canvassing: approximately one-fourth of the population of the northwest side of Chicago was contacted by telephone; Operation Breadbasket, under the leadership of the Rev. Jesse Jackson, canvassed the Southside wards. On election day, hundreds of lawyers served as poll watchers in most areas of Chicago, with the exception of the "river wards" which were considered by the campaign committee to be unassailable Democratic strongholds.

This extensive campaign in favor of merit selection of judges was not fought without strong opposition. There was extensive distribution of materials supporting the alternative proposition, the election of judges (option 2–A). Then, on November 30, Chicago Mayor Richard Daley officially endorsed the proposed constitution along with propositions 1–A and 2–A (cumulative voting and election of judges, respectively) and the proposition to lower the voting age to eighteen. With this endorsement of the retention of judicial election (rather than a switch to merit selection) the Democratic party faced a split in its ranks on what became the major issue of the campaign: U.S. Democratic Senator Stevenson and Democratic Lieutenant Governor Paul Simon had previously endorsed merit selection and locally, Rev. Jackson was attempting to pull black wards in Chicago away from the Democratic organization in support of merit appointment.

Some political observers believed the true test of Daley's strength in this election rested on the results of the separate question concerning the selection of judges rather than the constitution itself. Although Daley won the day, the score was not impressive. The organization mustered a slim 1.2-to-1 city-wide margin in favor of judicial election, losing thirteen wards to the alternative, and coming within 1,000 votes of losing in eight other wards. In only ten wards did proposition 2–A pick up a greater vote total than did the main document. In all but one of the black Democratic wards, the reverse was true although the diminished vote on this question was substantially in favor of election of judges. City areas which carried for judicial appointment were principally the Northside (Gold Coast) wards which also elect independent aldermen and some wards that may be labelled "weak" Democratic (for example, those wards where the margin of defeat in 1970 for Republican Ralph T. Smith in his Senate campaign against Democrat Adlai Stevenson III was less than two-to-one in a city which carried ten-to-one for Stevenson). These Chicago wards, coupled with a strong suburban vote for proposition 2–B, carried Cook County for judicial appointment.

The regional effect of the campaign for merit selections was indeed impressive. Six of the seven counties supporting judicial reform were clustered in the northeast corner of the state or roughly within the sphere of the 2–B campaign organization and its area of major activity. Nonetheless, the combined pluralities of the seven counties supporting judicial appointment were not sufficient to carry the state for proposition 2–B. In effect, the Chicago metropolitan area had been neutralized (city vs. suburbs) thus permitting downstate to defeat the judicial reform.

The downstate strategy lacked the vigor of the Chicago area effort. In addition to television advertisements, a flying squadron of six 2–B proponents representing religious, civil rights, and educational groups touched down at press conferences in five cities—St. Louis, Missouri, whose press is read by many west-central Illinois residents, Springfield, Peoria, Rock Island, and Rockford—on a two-day "2–B Truth Tour." The strategic objective was to discredit

Mayor Daley and by so doing establish an awareness among downstate voters—naturally hostile to Chicago politics—of the judicial selection battle lines and where the Democratic organization had thrown its weight.[4] It was hoped that downstate voters would follow their traditional inclination to oppose the Daley organization and vote for merit selection of judges, if only by negative impetus. The strategy did not work. Votes against 2–B averaged two and three to one. Proponents of 2–B had nonetheless raised a pre-election statewide survey figure of 24 percent in favor to the final level of 43 percent.

ABOLITION OF THE DEATH PENALTY (SEPARATE QUESTION NO. 3)

Although the campaign for single-member legislative districts was low-key of necessity, the campaign to abolish the death penalty was low-key by design. Developments nationwide and during the Illinois constitutional convention led at least one active pro-abolition delegate to conclude that there was latent public support for the removal of the death penalty. The strategy, then, became one of quietly arousing this support without, at the same time, stirring up substantial opposition.

The campaign developed essentially through the efforts of one delegate, Elmer Gertz, an independent from Chicago and chairman of the Bill of Rights Committee at the Convention. Office space was secured at the John Howard Association in Chicago. Board members included Clement Stone, Preston Bradley, Albert Jenner, Jr. and a number of similarly respected civic leaders. Funds of roughly $11,000, contributed primarily by Stone and the Hugh Hefner Foundation, were expended on literature which was distributed mainly in the Chicago area (although some downstate delegates distributed pamphlets in their districts) and media advertisements. The Hefner Foundation provided public relations assistance and a telephone brigade to assist in canvassing.

The campaign attempted to pull together three areas of support: the churches, blacks, and liberals. Unlike the campaign for the proposed constitution, this campaign placed heavy emphasis on the unstructured areas of potential electoral support. Its theme and tone were necessarily emotional and moralistic. Few newspapers, major organizations (with the exception of the Chicago Bar Association),

[4]Press package distributed by the Flying Squadron at press conferences throughout the state.

or political parties took a position on abolition of the death penalty. In fact, church hierarchies provided the only real pre-existing communications structures, and these were used extensively.

The assumptions, guesses, and strategies turned out to be wrong. On December 15, Illinois voters voted overwhelmingly in favor of retaining capital punishment (60.4 percent); only 33.5 percent voted to abolish it. This exceeded the division on all other issues voted upon at the election. Proponents of abolishing the death penalty were unprepared for so overwhelming a defeat. Early evidence had indicated a much closer election. Fifty-one percent of respondents to a survey one month prior to the election claimed they would vote for retaining the death penalty while 43 percent claimed they would vote for abolition. Six percent were undecided. Similarly, nationwide polls by the Harris, Gallup, and Roper organizations surveyed a growing feeling among people against this form of punishment, although this had not reached majority proportions. Most of these people felt the death penalty to be an ineffective means of deterring crime. Similarly, Illinois respondents to a 1969 opinion survey, who felt crime was a major state problem, did not believe capital punishment was any answer.[5] Only 18 percent felt stiff sentences were the solution to the increasing crime rate; 51 percent felt that enforcement of better laws was the answer. Despite these pre-election statistics, the post-election survey indicates that of the four separate submissions, respondents most often cited abolition of the death penalty, had it been in the main document, as unacceptable.

Gertz believes that the penalty would have been abolished if the Cook County Democratic organization and labor had endorsed this position rather than remaining neutral. However, it cannot be claimed that their neutrality cut into participation by voters on this question since 95.2 percent of those voting at the election voted on this issue. The black community of Chicago had overwhelmingly supported abolition. If the Democratic party had officially endorsed it, the vote ratio against abolition might have been different, but not to the degree necessary to carry the election. Cook County alone simply could not have secured passage of this proposition against the negative environment downstate.

[5] University of Illinois Survey Research Laboratory, *Mini-Omnibus Study #043* (Urbana, Illinois, spring 1969). Sample Size: 603

EIGHTEEN-YEAR-OLD VOTE (SEPARATE QUESTION NO. 4)

The eighteen-year-old vote had support from a wide range of organizations as well as both political parties. Even the AFL–CIO endorsed this particular constitutional issue, although it should be noted that they had not endorsed the proposed constitution. The success of this issue was ultimately linked to success of the "main package." Prior to convening of the convention, respondents to an opinion survey were asked whether they would approve of lowering the voting age: 57 percent replied "yes" and 39 percent said "no." Fifty-eight percent of the "yes" respondents explained their position with the popular argument, "if they are old enough to die for their country, they are old enough to vote." Of those against lowering the voting age, 76 percent felt eighteen-year-olds are not responsible or mature enough to vote.[6] In either case, emotion dominated reason. This fact coupled with the intensity with which people hold these views created a potentially explosive electoral situation.

To date, attempts in other states to lower the voting age had proved unsuccessful. Proposals to lower the voting age were rejected in eleven states where the question was on the November 1970 ballot. Interestingly, those states which did lower their voting age did so by dropping the requirement to twenty or nineteen years. However, 80 percent of the Illinois respondents who favored the lowered age requirement stood fast at eighteen years. Opponents were against any compromise.

The campaign for the eighteen-year-old vote in Illinois was fragmented and depended principally on local efforts by college and high school students. The state office of Project 18, a national group working for lowering the voting age, did not lend cohesion to these efforts.

Chicago area college students conducted one of the better organized college campaigns for lowering the voting age.[7] The campaign thrust was informational and students relied heavily upon a sympathetic news media to disseminate a prepared fact sheet. Approximately fifty-five managing editors of daily and weekly newspapers in Illinois received the fact sheet and/or were personally visited as were major radio and television stations throughout Chicago.

[6] Ibid.
[7] Memo from Davis L. Fisher, campaign organizer, dated December 21, 1970.

The fact sheets and roughly 112,000 copies of a "throw-away" pamphlet were made possible by a $1,000 contribution to the student campaign by the United Auto Workers. The handouts were distributed by students (recruited from a dozen Chicago and suburban high schools) on the Monday before the election at CTA stations, train depots, and on major streets in the Chicago Loop area. Front page coverage of the student effort was carried by the *Chicago Daily News* that evening.

These efforts, together with the Democratic party and AFL–CIO endorsements of the eighteen-year-old vote contributed to Cook County support on the issue. Cook was, however, the only county in the state to do so. Interestingly, throughout the state as a whole, only 43 percent of the voters cast their ballots in favor of the lowered voting age. Illinois joined the ranks of those states that had to wait for the 26th amendment to the constitution before their eighteen-year-olds were allowed to vote. The Illinois vote on the voting age requirement showed little variation between those counties hosting colleges and universities and those which do not, even though residents of the former were said to be especially fearful of college students dominating their local elections. An isolated comparison of votes favoring the lowered voting age between five major university towns and five neighboring, non-university towns of approximately equal size demonstrated greater support among the former (average of 47.6 percent to 37.4 percent) for the suffrage reform.[8] The presence of a generally less-conservative, university community was undeniably a factor contributing to these results.

The important feature of the defeat of the lowered voting age was the extensive—albeit perfunctory—organizational support of the eighteen-year-old vote spanning professional, educational, religious, business and labor groups as well as representatives of both major political parties. On this issue, at least, these groups were unable to affect the voting behavior of their memberships.

[8]Joan Severns, "A New Constitution for Illinois: Who Cares?" (unpublished paper, University of Illinois, 1971).

IX

Analysis of the Vote at the Ratifying Election

> We have won! There simply aren't enough people down-
> state to overcome these totals.
>
> Someone at campaign headquarters

At a special election on December 15, 1970, Illinois voters approved the new state constitution. Approximately 37 percent of the registered voters participated in the referendum. Of these, 1,122,425 (55.5 percent) voted for the constitution and 838,168 (42.0 percent) voted against. Separate submission of the four controversial issues helped passage of the 1970 constitution in more than one way. It discouraged the dangerous choice voters would otherwise have had to make between the entire work of the constitutional convention and one undesirable, potentially unacceptable, entry. Moreover, the additional interest stimulated by at least one mini-campaign caused more voters to support the main document. It had been feared, because several mini-campaigns emphasized their issue and not the constitution, that many voters would skip the main ballot question. However, voters realized the need to vote on the main document as well as on the separate questions, that passage of any of these items would be conditional upon passage of the constitution itself. Only 1.5 percent of the participants in the election did not vote on the main question.

On the major question statewide, the balance tipped favorably in behalf of constitutional reform. Cook County returns of two to one for ratification of the proposed constitution spelled victory early in the evening of December 15. Given a turnout of roughly twice as

TABLE I. SUMMARY OF VOTE ON BLUE BALLOT QUESTIONS
(Special Election, December 15, 1970)

Proposed constitution	
Yes	1,122,425
No	838,168
Election of representives from	
Option 1-A Multi-member districts by	
cumulative voting	1,031,241
Option 1-B Single-member districts	794,909
Selection of judges by	
Option 2-A Election	1,013,559
Option 2-B Appointment	867,230
Abolish death penalty	
Yes	676,302
No	1,218,791
Lower voting age to 18	
Yes	869,816
No	1,052,924

many registered Chicago area voters as downstate voters, and the absolute number of Chicago area voters (more than half the number voting at the election), one election observer felt confident to say, "We have won! There simply aren't enough people downstate to overcome these totals." The only serious downstate opposition came from Madison and St. Clair counties. As major southern population centers, these county results sliced heavily into the early victory margin. The East St. Louis metropolitan area voted 3.5 to one against the constitution.

The defeated structural reforms were heralded as "sacrificial lambs." Suffice it to say that the 1970 constitution would not have passed without Cook County Democratic party support, and it was by virtue of the separate submission of judicial selection, primarily, and legislative districts, secondarily, that the Democrats were able to offer their endorsement. It is ironic, therefore, that downstate saved judicial election, and not the Democrats themselves.

Although the legislative and judicial reforms failed to pass, voters nevertheless chose the 1970 structural refinements (the "A" options) over the so-called hidden third options, the relevant 1870 provisions, which would have been retained in the new constitution if the separately submitted items had failed to receive approval by a majority of those voting in the election. In short, a majority of Illinois voters preferred to correct deficiencies in their current forms of legislative and judicial selection (in the first case, insuring competition for seats in the lower house of the General Assembly and, in the second, replacing the party caucus method of nominating candidates for judicial office with direct primaries), rather than to change these facts of government altogether.

VOTING ON THE CONSTITUTION

Breakdown of the vote on the constitution reveals one striking feature about the election: the overwhelming support by Cook County voters carried the election in an otherwise lukewarm to negative environment. Downstate could not withstand the 350,000 Cook County plurality. Previously, Cook County "yes" votes on constitutional questions had been counterbalanced by downstate "no" votes or nonvotes. The impasse was broken only by the relative magnitude of these two opposing vote patterns. In this case, the negative response of seventy-two Illinois counties was insufficient to overcome the favorable support of the Chicago metropolitan area. Despite the lack of broad-based geographic support for the new Illinois charter, the thirty supporting counties nevertheless represent over 75 percent of the state's population.

Twenty-five of the thirty counties approving ratification had supported the constitutional convention call in November 1968. Five counties which had not supported the initial call for a convention did approve its final product. Inversely, twenty-eight counties which had supported the convention call did not endorse the proposed constitution. This was undoubtedly due to the fact that no specific issues were involved in the call campaign, the object being to determine whether or not to address the question of revision. However, the December referendum demanded endorsement by voters of substantive constitutional alterations and additions. Furthermore, twelve of these twenty-eight counties had in the past been quite negative on the question of constitutional amendments and were, therefore, merely assuming their traditional posture on such matters.[1] However, five counties similarly characterized as

[1]For further information on this point, see Thomas Kitsos, "Constitutional Amendments and the Voter, 1952–1966," Commission Papers of the Institute of Government and Public Affairs, University of Illinois (Urbana, 1968), p. 10. These counties had approved less than three of fifteen constitutional amendments presented to the voters in the period from 1952 to 1966.

"strongly negative" on the issue of reform defied their accustomed hostility toward constitutional revision by supporting both the convention call and ratification. All so-called favorable counties (those which had approved at least eight of 15 amendments in the 14-year-period between 1952 and 1966 supported the new state charter. Not surprisingly, the greater number of approving counties are "swing" areas, historically representing neither extreme of voting behavior (see Figure 1).

VOTING ON THE SEPARATE ISSUES

Disapproval by voters of the main document did not mean automatic disapproval of those separate items least resembling similar provisions in the 1870 constitution. Most striking was the support, measured in terms of number of counties, for a change in the method of selecting representatives to the lower house of the state legislature. Proposition 1–B, single-member districts for state representatives, a complete reversal of cumulative voting in multi-member districts (Option 1–A), was approved at this election in seventy-six Illinois counties. Hence a significant number of voters throughout the state supported the reform but not the package into which it would have to fit. Noteworthy, is the fact that numerous counties that supported this legislative reform have in the past been antagonistic toward constitutional amendments, including the amendments for legislative reapportionment and annual legislative sessions submitted to the voters in 1954 and 1964, respectively. Although only eight of the thirty counties voting for the constitution wanted to retain cumulative voting, one of these was Cook County and its 280,000 plurality for proposition 1–A was adequate to overcome wide geographic support for single-member legislative districts.

Option 2–B on judicial selection created what many believe to have been the driving force behind the relatively large turnout in Cook County on the blue ballot. Although the Cook County Democratic organization formally endorsed the proposed constitution, major emphasis was placed on proposition 2–A, the election of judges. To a degree, the attention by Democrats on this particular issue was forced by the well organized and financed counter-campaign for proposition 2–B, the appointment of judges. Using the structural remnants of Adlai Stevenson's November campaign organization in suburban Cook and the collar counties, 2–B propo-

FIGURE I. VOTER BEHAVIOR ON CONSTITUTIONAL QUESTIONS

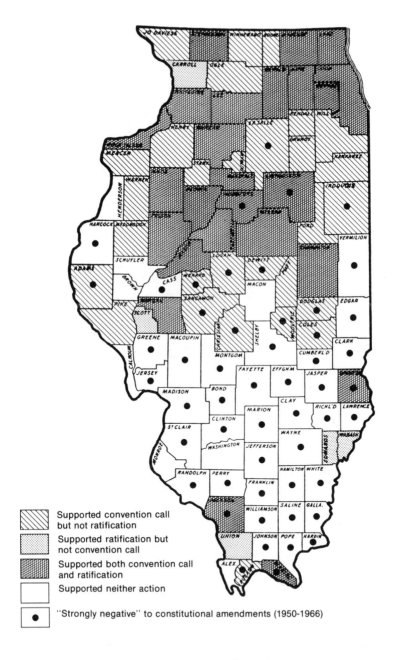

Supported convention call
but not ratification

Supported ratification but
not convention call

Supported both convention call
and ratification

Supported neither action

"Strongly negative" to constitutional amendments (1950-1966)

Source: JoAnna M. Watson, "Analysis of the Vote at the Election for the
1970 Illinois Constitution," *Illinois Government* 34 (February 1971).

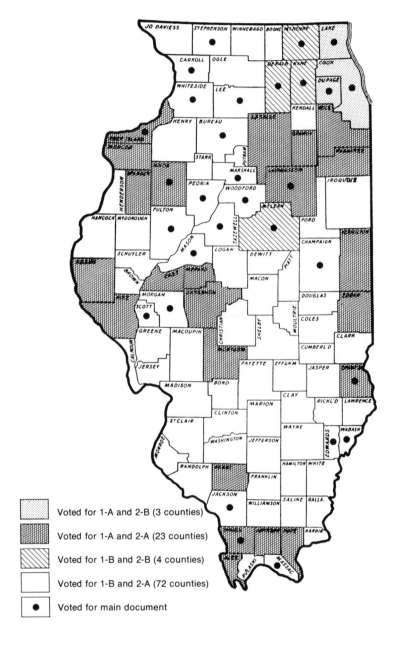

FIGURE II. BALLOT COMBINATIONS OF STRUCTURAL ISSUES
BY COUNTY

Voted for 1-A and 2-B (3 counties)

Voted for 1-A and 2-A (23 counties)

Voted for 1-B and 2-B (4 counties)

Voted for 1-B and 2-A (72 counties)

● Voted for main document

Source: JoAnna M. Watson, "Analysis of the Vote at the Election for the
1970 Illinois Constitution," *Illinois Government* 34 (February 1971).

nents pushed an impressive regional victory. However, the combined pluralities of the seven counties supporting judicial appointment were not sufficient to carry the state for option 2–B.

All four possible combinations of the legislative and judicial alternatives were evidenced statewide, although the most popular electoral combination was single-member legislative districts (1–B) with the election of judges (2–A). Seventy-two counties returned this pattern of essentially one structural reform and one retention. There was no relationship between support for the main package and the legislative reform. However, the four counties that returned favorable counts for both reform issues, options 1–B and 2–B, also supported the proposed constitution. Three counties, Cook, DuPage and Lake, voted the 1–A (multi-member districts) and 2–B (appointment of judges) combination. Twenty-three counties wanted to retain both multi-member districts and judicial election, the "A" options. Eighteen of these counties did not support the constitution (see Figure 2).

Frequently, county-wide approval of the new constitution hinged upon the relative turnout of urban and rural residents. Since urban areas throughout the state more strongly favored the document, a proportionately larger turnout by city voters at the December election usually carried their counties for the constitution. However, in counties where the rural vote exceeded or paralleled the average county turnout of registered voters, approval of the proposed constitution was less likely. Rarely did support by rural voters for the reform options of the four separate issues exceed support by urban voters. The cleavage is least marked in the vote for single-member legislative districts and greatest in the vote on the appointment of judges.

Voter Profile[2] survey data show that a majority of those voting either affirmatively or negatively on the proposed constitution in 1970 had approved the idea of a constitutional convention in 1968. Election returns indicate that counties which approved calling a constitutional convention in 1968 did not necessarily approve the product which emerged from the convention's deliberations. In fact, analysis of the 1968 vote reveals that there was no mandate as to type of revision sought by voters. The 54 percent of those voting against the constitution, having previously approved the convention call, apparently had in mind something more specific than simply "reform" or "modernization." Proponents for the new

[2]Geomedia, *Constitution Post-Election Study* (Chicago, Illinois, January 1971). Sample Size: 482

TABLE II. VOTING AT BOTH CONVENTION CALL AND
RATIFICATION ELECTIONS

	Had approved Convention Call	Had not approved Convention Call	Had not voted on question
Of those voting for the constitution	81%	2%	17%
Of those voting against the constitution (N = 482)	54%	30%	16%

constitution never once assumed or anticipated a momentum or carry-over from the 1968 victory. Nevertheless, a relationship between convention approval and affirmation of its product prevailed. Voters who had not participated on the question to call a convention were evenly split in their decision on the constitution. Those who voted at the delegate elections held in 1969 were equally split in their vote on the constitution. Groups who had opposed the convention and its product, such as the AFL–CIO, were, nevertheless, active in the delegate selection process. There is little reason for any significant relationship to have emerged between affirmative voting on the constitution and participation in the election of convention delegates.

When asked whether they felt the state needed a new constitution, 96 percent of "yes" voters on the constitution believed this to be the case, yet 56 percent of the "no" voters similarly felt the state needed a new constitution. This latter group, nevertheless, voted against the 1970 constitution either because the document did little to change the system in this state or because it did too much. In some cases, therefore, the new constitution lost in a race with the one-hundred-year-old constitution and, in others, it lost to a form of preconceived, ideal state constitution. Nineteen percent of the respondents felt the 1870 Illinois constitution did not require any revision at all. Downstate was particularly strong in this view.

Perhaps as a result of a three-year campaign by reformers to convince Illinois voters of *the need for a new constitution,* 77 percent of respondents who approved the new document gave "need" as reason for their action. When pressed for specifics, these voters most frequently mentioned "tax reform" as one of the best liked features of the new constitution. At the same time, the common reason given for voting against the constitution was, as it had been in the election to call a constitutional convention, a fear of resultant higher taxes.

Over half of those interviewed did not respond to the question on what aspect of the constitution they personally liked best.

Although it is difficult to distinguish voters at the constitutional referendum by their ascertainable positions, a tendency profile of voters for and against the constitution did emerge from the survey data.

TABLE III. TENDENCY PROFILE

Voters More Likely for Constitution	Voters More Likely Against Constitution
Men	Women
High school plus	High school and less
*Professional and white collar	Skilled blue collar & Service Occupations
Over $20,000	Under $7,000
Blacks	
(Middle income voters split)	

*Occupational distinctions are least marked.

In addition, political party affiliations bore some relationship to positive and negative voting behavior on the blue ballot in December 1970. As shown in Table IV, Democrats tended to favor the proposed constitution more often than did Republicans. It should be noted, however, that Chicago Democrats swelled the "yes" ranks while downstate Democrats voted more often against than for the constitution.

TABLE IV. POLITICAL PARTY AND CONSTITUTION VOTE

Party	Yes	No
Democratic	43%	31%
Republican	27	46
No affiliation	28	23
Not ascertained	2	—
(N = 482)	100	100

Furthermore, party affiliation seems to have affected voter opinions on whether the constitutional question or the section on separate submissions was the more important ballot issue. Chicago Mayor Daley was particularly concerned about the separate question on judicial selection and his Democratic ward leaders stressed that issue. Of the four separately submitted propositions, judicial selection was also the most important one for voters in Chicago—17 percent of survey respondents in Chicago as opposed to 5 percent downstate. State-wide, the eighteen-year-old vote was most often mentioned while legislative representation was least mentioned.

Geographic location also played a role. Table V shows that Chicago respondents were about equally divided on the alternatives offered by the four separately submitted items, whereas downstaters displayed strong preferences on at least three of the separate issues. Downstate metropolitan area respondents supported single-member districts and judicial election by ratios of two to one. Downstate rural areas were also strongly in favor of judicial election. Respondents to the survey were about equally divided statewide as to whether or not they approved the eighteen-year-old vote, although actual election returns showed the eighteen-year-old vote approved by a majority in only one county in the state.

TABLE V. GEOGRAPHIC AREAS AND VOTE ON SEPARATE ISSUES

	Chicago	Downstate Metropolitan	Downstate Non-Metropolitan
Single-member district	45%	62%	38%
Multi-member district	42	27	43
	87*	89	81
Appoint judges	46	27	15
Elect judges	50	68	85
	96	95	100
Abolish death penalty	43	35	30
Not abolish death penalty	53	62	56
	96	97	86
Lower voting age	42	42	50
Not Lower Voting age	55	58	50
	97	100	100

*Remainder didn't remember or didn't vote on that issue.

The survey data, as indicated by Table VI, reveal a relationship between income and a respondent's vote on the separately submitted questions. Only those with incomes above $15,000 tended to cast more votes for judicial appointment. Those with incomes under $7,000 were most in favor of abolishing the death penalty while middle income voters were most strongly opposed to this measure.

In other words, no one area of the state or particular income group favored all of the so-called reform alternatives (single-mem-

TABLE VI. INCOME AND VOTE ON SEPARATE ISSUES

	Under $7,000	$7,000 to $10,000	$10,000 to $15,000	Over $15,000
Single-member district	40%	61%	44%	42%
Multi-member district	33	29	45	53
	73*	90	89	95
Appoint judges	46	30	30	67
Elect judges	54	67	70	33
	100	97	100	100
Abolish death penalty	56	24	37	45
Not abolish death penalty	39	73	55	55
	95	97	92	100
Lower voting age	26	39	45	55
Not lower voting age	74	60	52	42
	100	99	97	97

*Remainder didn't remember or didn't vote on issue.

ber districts, judicial appointment, abolition of the death penalty and the eighteen-year-old vote). Similarly, no consistent pattern of total resistance to change emerged. It seems reasonable to suppose that the vote could be traced to how each respondent felt the outcome of the issue would affect his particular socioeconomic group. For example, it is popularly believed (a) that judicial appointment (the system set out by the convention delegates) would transfer the decision-making basis for selection of state judges from the masses to a political and professional elite; (b) that lower income groups suffer disproportionately under the death penalty while "middle America" perceives a further breakdown of law and order by limiting or abolishing its usage; and (c) that a lowered voting age will encourage the political activism of students principally from the "privileged" classes.

The survey data show a greater tendency among those voting "no" on the main document to resist the major revisions outlined in the separate provisions. The correlation was greatest on the proposition to lower the voting age and slightly less on the question of judicial selection (see Table VII). In all cases, proportionately more of those voting "yes" on the constitution supported the options reflecting greatest change within the system.

The question remains whether the constitution would have been defeated had no separate alternatives been offered the voters. Thirty percent of those voting "yes" on the constitution claimed they would have voted against it had the major revisions been included in the package. This was felt most strongly by Chicago respondents (34 percent) and least strongly by downstate rural respondents (5 percent). On the other hand, 18 percent of the "no" voters would have voted for the constitution had it been submitted as a whole with the reforms. Numerically, the exchange suggests a decreased chance for passage of the constitution. These figures, admittedly hypothetical, vindicate the Con Con delegates' decision to propose the separate submission of certain issues to the voters.

TABLE VII. VOTING ON SEPARATE ISSUES COMPARED TO VOTING ON CONSTITUTION

| | | Constitution | |
		Yes	No
Legislative districts	Single	48%	42%
	Multi	38	42
		86*	84
Judicial selection	Appoint	42	32
	Elect	54	67
		96	99
Death penalty	Abolish	46	31
	Not abolish	50	61
		96	92
Voting age	Lower	57	25
	Not lower	38	75
		95	100

*Remainder didn't remember or didn't vote on issue

Survey respondents were asked how they would have voted if the proposed revenue article and the 1870 revenue article had been offered as alternatives on a separate basis. A bare majority (51 percent) of those who approved the constitution claimed they would have voted for the new article while 42 percent would have voted to retain the 1870 article. Noteworthy is the number of people who voted for the constitution despite the new revenue article which they did not prefer. However, it is inconclusive whether the new revenue article alone turned numbers of voters away from supporting the main document as some campaign observers believed.

THE BLUE BALLOT NONVOTER

Sixty-two percent of qualified voters in Illinois did not participate at the election for adoption of the constitution. The survey data showed that nonvoters at the December 15 election tended to be occasional voters, if they were voters at all. Only 34 percent of these nonvoters claimed, in postelection interviews, to have voted in the November 1970 general elections, at which major state offices and congressional seats were contested. According to the survey, the voting record of those who did not participate in the December 15 election contrasts sharply with the record of those who did.

As indicated in Table VIII, 89 percent of 1970 blue ballot voters were consistent electoral participants while 53 percent of nonvoters participated in half or slightly less than half of all elections. General turnout figures would suggest that infrequent voters are more likely to vote at presidential elections and least likely to vote at referenda elections, whether local or statewide.

TABLE VIII. COMPARATIVE VOTING RECORDS OF BLUE BALLOT PARTICIPANTS AND NONPARTICIPANTS

Record	Nonvoter December 15, 1970	Voter December 15, 1970
Always vote	3%	36%
Vote in nearly all elections	40	53
	43%	89%
Vote in over half	19	6
Vote in less than half	34	3
	53	9
Not answering	4	2
	100	100

Our general data confirmed this pattern. The record of 1970 referendum nonvoters reveals that: 46 percent of them failed to vote in the 1970 general election; 66 percent of them did not participate in the delegate elections of 1969; yet only 13 percent did not vote in the 1968 presidential election.

Demographically, the 1970 blue ballot nonvoter was unlike the voter in a number of ways: he was younger (Table IX), had less education (Table X), was more likely to be a blue-collar worker (Table XI), made less than $10,000 annually (Table XII), and was less likely to own a home (Table XIII). Furthermore, with the exception of party affiliation, in which nonvoters and "yes" voters were more likely than "no" voters to be Democrats (Table XIV), the nonvoters did not more closely resemble one or the other of the voting populations. It should also be pointed out that the data on party affiliation suggest that without the influence exerted by the Chicago Democratic organization upon its voters (especially blacks), the distinc-

TABLE IX. AGE AND VOTING BEHAVIOR
(December 15, 1970)

| | | On Constitution | |
	Nonvoters	Yes Voters	No Voters
21-29	23%	13%	9%
30-39	22	12	25
40-55	28	47	31
Over 55	27	28	36
	100	100	100

TABLE X. EDUCATION AND VOTING BEHAVIOR
(December 15, 1970)

| | | On Constitution | |
	Nonvoters	Yes Voters	No Voters
No School	4%	0%	0%
Grade School	14	7	10
Some High School	22	10	8
Grad. High School	26	32	52
Some College	15	17	19
Grad. College	8	21	7
Grad. Work	6	4	0
Not Answering	5	9	4
	100	100	100

TABLE XI. OCCUPATION AND VOTING BEHAVIOR
(December 15, 1970)

| | | On Constitution | |
	Nonvoters	Yes Voters	No Voters
Professional (Proprietors, mgrs.)	13%	27%	18%
Clerical-sales	13	11	8
Skilled Blue	9	5	3
Service	5	3	4
Other Blue	11	9	8
Farm	2	1	4
Unemployed	2	—	—
Not in labor force	40	39	49
Not Answering	5	5	7
	100	100	100

TABLE XII. INCOME AND VOTING BEHAVIOR
(December 15, 1970)

| | | On Constitution | |
	Nonvoters	Yes Voters	No Voters
Under $7,000	31%	8%	16%
$7,000–$10,000	20	20	20
$10,000–$15,000	24	28	45
Over $15,000	13	15	9
Not Answering	12	29	10
	100	100	100

TABLE XIII. HOUSING AND VOTING BEHAVIOR
(December 15, 1970)

| | | On Constitution | |
	Nonvoters	Yes Voters	No Voters
Own	65%	79%	86
Rent	34	14	12
Not Answering	1	7	2
	100	100	100

TABLE XIV. PARTY AFFILIATION AND VOTING BEHAVIOR
(December 15, 1970)

| | | On Constitution | |
	Nonvoters	"Yes" Voters	"No" Voters
Democrat			
Strong	10%	10%	9%
Lean	44	34	23
Republican			
Strong	4	4	5
Lean	19	23	40
Not Answering	23	29	23
	100	100	100

tions between referendum voters and nonvoters would have been clearer.

Although nonvoters did not choose to express their views by voting at the special election, they were not without opinions about

TABLE XV. EDUCATION, INCOME, AND VOTING BEHAVIOR*

| | | On Constitution | |
	Nonvoters	"Yes" Voters	"No" Voters
Educational Attainment			
None to some high school	40%	17%	18%
College graduate plus	14	25	7
Annual Income			
Less than $10,000	51	28	36
More than $10,000	37	43	54

*Note that according to Tables X and XII more "yes" voters did not respond to these questions.

the proposed constitution and the alternative propositions. The survey data revealed that 76 percent of all those who did not vote believed the state needed a new constitution, but would not have voted on the separate questions as did those who claimed they had voted. They were more strongly opposed to judicial appointment, in favor of the eighteen-year-old vote, and less likely to support single-member legislative districts.

TABLE XVI. HOW WOULD (DID) YOU VOTE ON THE SEPARATE ISSUES?

Options	Nonvoters	Voters
Legislative Districts		
Single-member	36%	45%
Multi-member	39	40
Not answering/don't remember	25	15
Judicial Selection		
Appointment	22	38
Election	74	60
Not answering/don't remember	4	2
Death Penalty		
Abolish	40	39
Not Abolish	54	55
Not answering/don't remember	6	6
Lower Vote Age (18)		
Lower	57	43
Not Lower	41	54
Not answering/don't remember	2	3

Nonvoters were less aware of campaign events than were voters. Few nonvoters mentioned the news media as an informational source. Sources of influence were further restricted by the fact that half as many nonvoters as voters belong to social, occupational, or cultural/hobby organizations which disseminated a significant portion of the campaign literature. Roughly half as many possessed any knowledge of political party endorsements. Yet, 57 percent of the nonvoters surveyed claimed they "knew" there was an election for adoption of a new Illinois constitution. Only five percent said they did not vote because they had forgotten. Major reasons for not voting were: Not interested, 23 percent; too busy, 23 percent; not registered, 20 percent; other (e.g., illness, death in family), 30 percent; and not answering, 4 percent. Apathy or indifference accounts for the behavior of many nonvoters. Sixty-eight percent consider themselves a part of the "silent majority," defined as a group of individuals who are primarily not vocal or not interested in politics.

There exist at least three other plausible reasons for voter nonparticipation at the constitutional election: (1) political alienation; (2) personal relevance; and (3) electoral priority. First, the degree of political alienation among nonvoters was greater than that among blue ballot voters. Respondents were asked either to agree or disagree with five statements designed to measure a sense of political efficacy. Agreement implied a sense of political frustration and/or distrust.

TABLE XVII. POLITICAL EFFICACY AND CONSTITUTIONAL VOTE

Statement Responses	Nonvoters	Yes Voters	No Voters
Set 1*—Efficacy	46%	58%	47%
Set 2**—Powerlessness	54	42	53
	100	100	100

*Set 1—Agreement with none, one or two statements.
**Set 2—Agreement with three, four or all five statements.[3]

A sense of political efficacy was strongest among constitutional "yes" voters as shown in Table XVII. Note, however, the similarity of responses between "no" voters and nonvoters. These results support the proposition that the politically alienated may react in either of these fashions.

[3] These statements were directly related to income: of those agreeing with three, four or all five (powerlessness), 77 percent earned less than $7,000; $7,000 to $10,000, 56 percent; $10,000 to $15,000, 44 percent; over $15,000, 35 percent.

Second, it is not likely that nonvoters were primarily conservative and resisted change or were satisfied with things, principally economic, as they existed. Twice as many nonvoters as voters claimed their families were "worse off" that year compared to the previous year. It is more likely that nonvoters did not see state constitutional revision as a way of changing matters relating to themselves. However, nearly a majority of these same respondents were in favor of calling a convention to review the U.S. Constitution; majorities of both "yes" and "no" voters on the state constitution were opposed to such action on the national level.

TABLE XVIII. DESIRE FOR U.S. CONSTITUTIONAL REVIEW

Position	Nonvoters	Yes Voters	No Voters
For review	49%	22%	33%
Against review	43	72	58
No opinion	8	6	9
	100	100	100

In terms of relevance, therefore, one might conclude that many citizens see the federal government, and not the states, as the locus for economic and social reform in this country.

In terms of electoral priority, it must be remembered that the nonvoters at this particular election are not consistent electoral participants and are least likely to vote in elections of this nature. They predictably place less value upon state and local referenda than do blue ballot voters. When asked whether they felt the constitutional referendum was more important than U.S. senatorial elections, 47 percent of the nonvoters agreed whereas the response by voters was 67 percent.

In summary, the survey data demonstrate a latent source of support for the 1970 Illinois Constitution among respondents who—for whatever reason—did not vote at the December 15 election. Three-quarters of these nonvoting respondents believed in the need for constitutional revision. They were not nonparticipants because they were unaware or even undecided about the issues. Rather, they did not have the impetus to vote. This was partially the result of the low-key campaign waged for acceptance of the constitution and partially a reflection of the nature of their own voting habits.

The affirmative voter at this election appeared to know less about the constitution and endorsing individuals and organizations than did the negative voter. The latter was better able to "explain" his vote and was aware of groups with whom he did not agree on the constitutional questions. Roughly half of those who voted "no" claimed to have been undecided about the issue for at least a portion of the thirteen-week campaign. On the other hand, an overwhelming number of blue ballot "yes" voters had been a consistent source of support for constitutional revision. If anything, the campaign provided reinforcement for existing beliefs. Theirs was not an electoral decision based upon campaign events (e.g., endorsements). Consequently, fewer could articulate their reasons for voting as they did. Instead, they dwelt at length on slogans—the modernization themes—which had sustained them throughout the three-year effort to revise the constitution.

* * * * * * * * * * *

The success of constitutional revision is measured first by the election results. Later, its provisions will be tested—its protection of human rights, its home rule for cities, its tax limitations, and so forth. These and other matters will be the source of discussion for years to come.[4] Problems will be identified and adjustments demanded for shifting needs. For this reason the 1970 constitution requires an automatic convention call every twenty years. Thus the ongoing process of constitutional review in Illinois is ensured, and future generations of Illinois citizens are released from mounting the critical first step. Today's groundwork will trigger tomorrow's constitutional examination.

At the same time, future revisions may never again reflect so clearly the civic spirit that went into the making of the 1970 constitution. For there is no denying that the burden of the preliminary effort to focus attention on the need for constitutional reform and the success of that revision must be placed with the citizens of this state. Into the hands of private citizens, for the most part, fell the task of generating the reform movement, of grabbing any opportunity to facilitate the electoral process, and of bringing the constitutional endeavor to its successful conclusion. It is most fitting that this most public of documents should have its roots deep in the minds and labor of private, yet public-spirited, citizens.

---

[4] For one example of such a study, see Samuel Witwer, "Preface Symposium: the 1970 Illinois Constitution," *John Marshall Journal of Practice and Procedure* 11, no. 2 (winter 1977–78): 254.

Appendix A

VOTE FOR THE PROPOSITION OF CALLING A CONSTITUTIONAL CONVENTION—NOVEMBER 5, 1968

Counties	Total Vote	Yes	No
Adams	32,367	16,191	10,979
Alexander	7,065	2,397	1,664
Bond	7,074	2,957	2,185
Boone	9,737	5,811	3,926
Brown	3,225	1,163	1,980
Bureau	18,873	10,372	6,461
Calhoun	3,214	1,244	820
Carroll	8,360	3,820	3,328
Cass	7,221	3,916	2,623
Champaign	49,965	33,644	11,448
Christian	18,028	9,956	5,564
Clark	8,716	4,153	2,962
Clay	8,105	3,408	2,603
Clinton	12,245	4,719	5,095
Coles	19,977	10,000	7,720
Cook	(See below)		
Crawford	10,154	5,934	2,636
Cumberland	5,100	2,159	2,143
DeKalb	23,457	16,146	5,037
DeWitt	8,451	4,331	2,865
Douglas	8,579	4,337	3,309
DuPage	187,584	133,284	48,440
Edgar	11,317	5,139	6,191
Edwards	4,219	1,852	993
Effingham	12,176	5,632	4,568
Fayette	10,559	3,818	4,608
Ford	8,074	4,688	2,341
Franklin	21,558	6,856	6,166
Fulton	20,773	12,329	6,746
Gallatin	4,252	1,482	1,492
Greene	7,797	3,312	3,495
Grundy	11,187	6,748	3,505
Hamilton	5,550	1,556	1,896
Hancock	11,533	5,494	4,112
Hardin	2,966	840	1,652
Henderson	4,166	1,959	1,460
Henry	23,142	14,507	5,939
Iroquois	16,175	8,378	5,318
Jackson	19,972	10,618	9,072
Jasper	5,790	2,426	2,165
Jefferson	15,717	4,733	7,886
Jersey	8,245	2,951	3,684
JoDaviess	9,467	5,540	2,480
Johnson	4,061	1,356	1,335
Kane	88,733	58,608	20,950
Kankakee	38,581	22,432	10,698
Kendall	10,276	5,775	3,783
Knox	27,060	14,702	7,930
Lake	127,904	84,105	31,839
LaSalle	52,233	27,673	16,853
Lawrence	9,117	4,098	3,138
Lee	15,375	8,481	5,820
Livingston	18,293	11,277	4,952
Logan	14,407	7,850	4,328
Macon	51,790	33,752	12,336
Macoupin	23,759	9,602	12,171
Madison	102,057	42,661	43,195
Marion	18,573	5,853	7,859
Marshall	6,746	4,237	1,792
Mason	7,930	4,762	2,370

Source: Official Vote at General Election, November 5, 1968, pp. 50–51.

**VOTE FOR THE PROPOSITION OF CALLING A CONSTITUTIONAL
CONVENTION—NOVEMBER 5, 1968—Concluded**

Counties	Total Vote	Yes	No
Massac	6,555	2,374	1,721
McDonough	13,003	7,683	3,720
McHenry	43,222	27,242	10,783
McLean	38,678	24,124	12,070
Menard	5,049	2,743	1,906
Mercer	8,594	5,140	2,475
Monroe	9,387	4,614	3,153
Montgomery	16,580	6,218	6,939
Morgan	16,450	11,224	3,470
Moultrie	6,251	3,191	2,180
Ogle	17,734	9,248	6,650
Peoria	78,284	46,701	18,387
Perry	11,116	4,059	3,687
Piatt	7,080	3,875	2,745
Pike	10,101	5,220	3,405
Pope	2,323	734	881
Pulaski	4,765	1,615	981
Putnam	2,537	1,319	743
Randolph	15,390	6,714	4,829
Richland	8,301	4,048	2,418
Rock Island	71,585	48,674	20,133
Saline	14,169	6,167	3,586
Sangamon	76,468	39,925	21,876
Schuyler	4,681	1,546	2,524
Scott	3,620	1,791	1,187
Shelby	11,327	5,318	4,338
Stark	3,679	2,401	860
St. Clair	102,385	40,258	33,922
Stephenson	20,047	12,264	6,519
Tazewell	48,954	30,588	13,765
Union	8,499	3,140	2,388
Vermilion	43,797	19,892	17,383
Wabash	6,464	2,917	1,777
Warren	9,849	5,156	3,370
Washington	7,673	2,835	3,073
Wayne	9,440	3,239	3,937
White	10,106	4,022	3,974
Whiteside	24,739	12,896	8,592
Will	91,791	55,480	23,129
Williamson	23,768	5,646	9,121
Winnebago	93,342	56,104	27,394
Woodford	12,831	7,770	3,250
Down State	2,329,641	1,284,139	720,147
Cook County	2,376,211	1,695,838	415,293
Total	4,705,852	2,979,977	1,135,440

In order for the Proposed Constitution Convention to pass the proposition must receive a majority of those voting at the election.

Appendix B

Counties	Total Vote	Counties	Total Vote
Adams	7,778	Macoupin	8,528
Alexander	1,143	Madison	13,335
Bond	850	Marion	4,371
Boone	1,952	Marshall	1,462
Brown	766	Mason	1,771
Bureau	4,491	Massac	484
Calhoun	1,012	McDonough	1,558
Carroll	2,775	McHenry	8,949
Cass	1,254	McLean	7,051
Champaign	8,908	Menard	1,616
Christian	2,175	Mercer	1,625
Clark	1,229	Monroe	1,181
Clay	1,654	Montgomery	3,541
Clinton	2,052	Morgan	4,778
Coles	4,203	Moultrie	1,575
Cook	531,115	Ogle	4,439
Crawford	2,286	Peoria (For 42nd Dist. Only)	590
Cumberland	791	Perry	2,741
DeKalb	6,180	Piatt	1,423
DeWitt	1,449	Pike	1,861
Douglas	1,449	Pope	546
DuPage	37,443	Pulaski	552
Edgar	2,225	Putnam	555
Edwards	1,808	Randolph	2,123
Effingham	3,377	Richland	1,245
Fayette	1,830	Rock Island	11,807
Ford	1,551	Saline	2,490
Franklin	3,885	Sangamon	26,626
Fulton	3,582	Schuyler	700
Gallatin	881	Scott	668
Greene	1,003	Shelby	2,222
Grundy	1,950	Stark (No Primary)	....
Hamilton	833	St. Clair	14,979
Hancock	1,788	Stephenson	5,486
Hardin	381	Tazewell	7,331
Henderson	593	Union	1,218
Henry	4,791	Vermilion	7,815
Iroquois	4,598	Wabash	1,302
Jackson	3,160	Warren	2,830
Jasper	1,039	Washington	1,327
Jefferson	3,377	Wayne	1,640
Jersey	2,447	White	1,466
JoDaviess	2,892	Whiteside	5,827
Johnson	610	Will	16,855
Kane	20,057	Williamson	4,029
Kankakee	10,103	Winnebago	15,017
Kendall	2,920	Woodford	2,845
Knox	5,142		
Lake	29,232		
LaSalle	9,136	Total	982,438
Lawrence	1,706		
Lee	4,137		
Livingston	3,314		
Logan	4,503		
Macon	8,252		

Source: Official Vote at General Election, November 3, 1970, pp. 76–79.

PRIMARY VOTE FOR MEMBERS OF THE CONSTITUTIONAL CONVENTION—SEPTEMBER 23, 1969

1st District—Cook County

Samuel W. Witwer	20,347
Frank Cicero, Jr	11,870
Marion E. Burks	8,205
Joseph W. Smith	3,991
Steven J. Schada	3,848
Robert A. Simon	3,394
Robert J. Salberg	908

2nd District—Cook County

Lucy Reum	8,609
Thomas J. McCracken	8,112
John J. Walsh, Jr	6,451
Arthur J. Moore, Jr	5,638
Thomas Campbell	3,858
Jack C. Rossetter	3,731
Dwight W. Follett	3,679
Michael W. Miela	1,630
Reginald A. Barnett	1,394
Melvin R. Kurr	405

3rd District—Cook County

John G. Woods	9,069
Virginia B. MacDonald	8,649
William R. Engelhardt	5,576
Madeline Schroeder	5,484
Mary Jordan Carlson	3,611
Eugene L. Griffin	2,256
Thomas J. Johnson, Jr	1,943
Samuel A. LaSusa	1,181
Wilfred L. Robbins	1,125
Douglas Roy Cannon	1,016
LeMoine D. Stitt, Jr	927
Lester A. Bonaguro	875
Robert A. Bush	722
Donald F. Colby	721
Winn C. Davidson	631
Annis F. Bush	440

4th District—Cook County

Marshall S. Howard	9,051
Clyde Parker	8,332
Anne H. Evans	8,090
Theodore A. Shapero	4,723
Michael Howard Lavin	4,716
Samuel T. Cohen	1,893
Jerome Goldstick	1,825
William C. Nigut	1,734
Franklin Lee	767
James I. Gottreich	666

5th District—Cook County

John E. Dvorak	6,585
Dr. Robert N. Price	5,133
Samuel A. DeCaro	4,991
Anne Willer	4,613
Vernon R. Forgue	4,475
Mary A. O'Callaghan	3,720
Raymond G. Cox	3,178
Thomas V. Kane	2,667
Gorden H. Ryan	1,912
Luella M. Seida	1,354
Kirby Johnston	573
Write-ins	2

6th District—Cook County

Martin Ozinga, Jr	8,455
Porter Orr	4,698
James E. Gierach	4,345
Herbert V. Huskey	2,873
Jean A. Keeney	2,776
Bill P. Perry	2,420
Lester F. Catlin	1,989
Richard O. Bennett	1,965
Frank McCune	1,903
Robert G. Johannsen	1,435
Ralph J. Berg	1,203
Lester D. McCurrie	668
Sandra J. Stegenga	641
Joan A. Plahm	549
Z. Erol Smith	519
Roy C. Johnson	304
James Edward Jones	294
Jordan Morris	240

7th District—Cook County

Joseph A. Tecson	14,130
Roy C. Pechous	13,966
Gerald W. Shea	8,201
Frederick C. Smith	6,435
George Eugene Sorini	2,548
Stanley Francis Rocush	2,146
M. Roy Murray	1,708
Write-ins	4

8th District—Cook County

Ray H. Garrison	7,567
Mary Lee Inger	7,474
Gerald W. Getty	5,129
Thomas H. Miller	4,054
Berniece P. Taylor	2,221
Samuel LaPorte, Jr	1,484
Robert L. Ryan	1,451
Ronald J. Kolodziej	925
Lawrence F. Kast	817
Diane E. Kreiman	602
Harlan G. Bogie	508
Emmajean Hemingway	426

9th District—Cook County

Joan G. Anderson	5,577
Terrel E. Clarke	5,121
Joseph T. Meek	4,655
William E. Cairnes	2,673
Jennifer E. Hance	2,605
Harry Raday	2,539
Bruno L. Sendera	2,246
Ollie E. Stone	1,822
Richard C. Reinke	1,714
Stewart M. Loebe	837
Marvin C. Chandler	580
Edward R. Zwicker	344
Patrick Joseph Lehnerer	304

10th District—Cook County

Esther Saperstein	13,842
Peter Andrew Tomei	13,165
Paul F. Elward	12,016
Peggy S. Norton	7,208
Mary Liguori Brophy	2,879
John D. O'Hara	2,460
Nathan Hoffberg	2,130
Mons H. Sebby	930

PRIMARY VOTE FOR MEMBER OF THE CONSTITUTIONAL CONVENTION—SEPTEMBER 23, 1969—(Continued)

11TH DISTRICT—COOK COUNTY

Martin Tuchow	10,065
Bernard Weisberg	9,950
Thomas J. Heneghan	8,369
Bennett B. Harvey, Jr.	5,104
Edith D. Graham	4,558
Neal Ball	4,472
Lawrence M. Mages	677
Philip A. Tunis	602

12TH DISTRICT—COOK COUNTY

Dawn Clark Netsch	13,834
Malcolm S. Kamin	12,153
Albert W. Hachmeister	4,983
John A. Kearney	4,413
Elroy C. Sandquist, Jr.	4,339
Theodore Pearson	910
Ronald W. Olson	710

13TH DISTRICT—COOK COUNTY

John C. Geocaris	10,662
Jack DeMichaels	10,168
Ronald C. Smith	6,794
Elmer Gertz	6,528
Raymond H. Schumacher	6,116
Sherwin H. Bender	3,132
Thomas Clyne Brophy	1,367
Mary Ann Fogarty	1,210
John J. Hogan	855
Harry P. Kuhr	380

14TH DISTRICT—COOK COUNTY

John F. Leon	10,126
William J. Laurino	9,865
Vincent J. Poklacki	4,082
Roger H. L. C. Charlier	4,041
Leon S. Conlon	2,577
Stephen J. Telow	1,765
Fred H. Justin, Jr.	1,220

15TH DISTRICT—COOK COUNTY

Thomas G. Lyons	19,383
David E. Stahl	18,179
Zeamore A. Ader	4,630
Edward R. Burr	2,967
Ken Denzel	2,946
Joseph M. Moran	2,328
Melbourne A. Noel, Jr.	2,001

16TH DISTRICT—COOK COUNTY

William F. Lennon	12,770
James E. Strunck	12,435
Catherine M. Richards	6,289
Donald Farrell Eslick	4,962
Joseph S. Zukowski	4,018
Robert Joseph Kennedy	2,949
Frank Haluska	1,903
Samuel J. Deitch	1,658
Monica R. Garstka	1,172
Timothy J. Sullivan	1,080
Joseph Louis Rispoli	888
Robert E. Romano	788
Kenneth P. Gill	759
Warren M. Mose	556

17TH DISTRICT—COOK COUNTY

Harold M. Nudelman	18,558
Frank Orlando	16,263
Harry Axelrod	3,578
Thomas E. Kramer	3,154
Henry L. Klinger	2,033
Leo R. Granger	1,335

18TH DISTRICT—COOK COUNTY

Edward J. Rosewell	11,224
Leonard N. Foster	9,789
Edward L. Stepnowski	2,655
Howard A. Heldt	2,251
Alfred L. Portis	2,174
LeRoy Cross	1,731
Write-ins	1

19TH DISTRICT—COOK COUNTY
No Primary Held

20TH DISTRICT—COOK COUNTY
No Primary Held

21ST DISTRICT—COOK COUNTY
No Primary Held

22ND DISTRICT—COOK COUNTY
No Primary Held

23RD DISTRICT—COOK COUNTY

Richard M. Daley	24,436
Leonard F. Miska	20,714
John P. Tully	4,027
Robert A. Urbanek	3,311
George E. Esch	2,001
Howard J. Doyle	1,305
Stephen J. Winbush	821
Write-ins	70

24TH DISTRICT—COOK COUNTY

Odas Nicholson	9,180
Albert A. Raby	9,044
Michael L. Shakman	7,677
Attye Belle McGee	6,736
Noble W. Lee	3,709
Robert H. Engle	1,070
Edwin H. Conger	824
Bobby R. Moss	754

25TH DISTRICT—COOK COUNTY

Francis X. Lawlor	18,159
Gabriel J. Barrett	11,152
Stanley A. Papierz	9,484
Louis Marolda	8,591
John J. Pempek	3,493
Daniel J. Kwiat	3,181
Leo W. Anderson	1,543
Kenneth J. Prokop	1,518

26TH DISTRICT—COOK COUNTY
No Primary Held

PRIMARY VOTE FOR MEMBER OF THE CONSTITUTIONAL CONVENTION—SEPTEMBER 23, 1969 —(Continued)

27TH DISTRICT—COOK COUNTY		29TH DISTRICT—COOK COUNTY	
No Primary Held		No Primary Held	
28TH DISTRICT—COOK COUNTY		30TH DISTRICT—COOK COUNTY	
Philip J. Carey	8,830	Henry M. Soltysinski	9,642
Ted A. Borek	7,760	David Linn	9,115
Lendol D. Snow	7,024	Mary Lee Leahy	5,542
Edward P. Sheridan	6,506	John Chico	5,267
Karen L. Mansfield	3,257	Joseph A. Grande	4,519
William A. Heatherly	2,805	Dorothy Lois Stevenson	3,148
Daniel O. Murray	2,438	Dr. Arnold J. Kuhn	1,647
Peter D. Oosterbaan	1,319	Zeno Thigpen	1,136
John D. Gottlick	1,275	Irwin Hirsch	933
Carl J. Ferraro	1,248		
Casimir G. Oksas	856		
Write-ins	1		

Appendix C

Counties	Total Vote	Counties	Total Vote
Adams	9,895	Macoupin	9,178
Alexander	749	Madison	15,516
Bond	1,168	Marion	5,741
Boone	2,032	Marshall	1,653
Brown	984	Mason	2,273
Bureau	6,598	Massac	685
Calhoun	960	McDonough	2,433
Carroll	3,446	McHenry	14,550
Cass	1,696	McLean	11,030
Champaign	14,413	Menard	2,194
Christian	3,603	Mercer	2,241
Clark	1,567	Monroe	1,716
Clay	2,061	Montgomery	4,593
Clinton	2,611	Morgan	5,973
Coles	5,955	Moultrie	2,144
Cook	827,141	Ogle	5,110
Crawford	2,962	Peoria	16,300
Cumberland	948	Perry	3,944
DeKalb	8,123	Piatt	1,993
DeWitt	1,904	Pike	2,122
Douglas	2,289	Pope	564
DuPage	50,308	Pulaski	1,012
Edgar	3,889	Putnam	676
Edwards	2,325	Randolph	3,817
Effingham	4,110	Richland	1,586
Fayette	2,632	Rock Island	17,975
Ford	2,213	Saline	2,743
Franklin	5,401	Sangamon	27,974
Fulton	4,415	Schuyler	1,036
Gallatin	1,139	Scott	811
Greene	1,233	Shelby	3,491
Grundy	2,968	Stark	820
Hamilton	1,129	St. Clair	17,943
Hancock	2,529	Stephenson	6,675
Hardin	442	Tazewell	11,323
Henderson	987	Union	1,572
Henry	6,824	Vermilion	10,974
Iroquois	5,695	Wabash	1,489
Jackson	4,018	Warren	3,725
Jasper	1,359	Washington	2,145
Jefferson	4,366	Wayne	2,674
Jersey	1,624	White	1,742
JoDaviess	3,440	Whiteside	6,642
Johnson	840	Will	24,009
Kane	31,058	Williamson	5,688
Kankakee	14,586	Winnebago	21,711
Kendall	3,635	Woodford	3,460
Knox	6,022		
Lake	37,310		
LaSalle	11,453		
Lawrence	1,808	Total	1,442,314
Lee	4,142		
Livingston	4,921		
Logan	6,052		
Macon	10,670		

Source: Official Vote at General Election, November 3, 1970, pp. 91–100.

VOTE FOR MEMBERS OF THE CONSTITUTIONAL CONVENTION
GENERAL ELECTION—NOVEMBER 18, 1969—(Continued)

1ST DISTRICT—COOK COUNTY

Samuel W. Witwer	30,677
Frank Cicero, Jr.	20,369
Marion E. Burks	13,781
Joseph W. Smith	6,280
Write-ins	3

2ND DISTRICT—COOK COUNTY

Lucy Reum	15,925
Thomas J. McCracken	14,721
John J. Walsh, Jr.	12,832
Arthur J. Moore, Jr.	8,570
Write-ins	2

3RD DISTRICT—COOK COUNTY

John G. Woods	19,807
Virginia B. MacDonald	17,202
Madeline Schroeder	13,112
William R. Engelhardt	9,429

4TH DISTRICT—COOK COUNTY

Anne H. Evans	16,033
Clyde Parker	15,857
Marshall S. Howard	14,026
Theodore A. Shapero	10,064
Write-ins	6

5TH DISTRICT—COOK COUNTY

John E. Dvorak	14,065
Anne Willer	13,017
Dr. Robert N. Price	12,005
Samuel A. DeCaro	10,437

6TH DISTRICT—COOK COUNTY

Martin Ozinga, Jr.	15,232
James E. Gierach	14,496
Herbert V. Huskey	14,012
Porter Orr	12,465

7TH DISTRICT—COOK COUNTY

Joseph A. Tecson	22,895
Roy C. Pechous	22,093
Gerald W. Shea	14,858
Frederick C. Smith	10,001
Write-ins	8

8TH DISTRICT—COOK COUNTY

Ray H. Garrison	14,613
Thomas H. Miller	11,896
Mary Lee Inger	10,911
Gerald W. Getty	8,085

9TH DISTRICT—COOK COUNTY

Joan G. Anderson	13,680
Joseph T. Meek	11,605
Terrel E. Clarke	7,678
William E. Cairnes	5,671
Write-ins	1

10TH DISTRICT—COOK COUNTY

Peter Andrew Tomei	24,961
Paul F. Elward	19,744
Esther Saperstein	19,590
Peggy S. Norton	16,175
Write-ins	2

11TH DISTRICT—COOK COUNTY

Bernard Weisberg	15,535
Martin Tuchow	13,520
Thomas J. Heneghan	13,134
Bennet B. Harvey, Jr.	12,889
Write-ins	2

12TH DISTRICT—COOK COUNTY

Dawn Clark Netsch	18,743
Malcolm S. Kamin	14,766
John A. Kearney	7,949
Albert W. Hachmeister	7,417

13TH DISTRICT—COOK COUNTY

Elmer Gertz	16,031
Ronald C. Smith	15,920
John C. Geocaris	15,701
Jack DeMichaels	15,085

14TH DISTRICT—COOK COUNTY

John F. Leon	14,447
William J. Laurino	13,865
Vincent J. Poklacki	8,540
Roger H. L. C. Charlier	7,301

15TH DISTRICT—COOK COUNTY

Thomas G. Lyons	26,646
David E. Stahl	25,767
Zeamore A. Ader	8,356
Edward R. Burr	6,122

16TH DISTRICT—COOK COUNTY

William F. Lennon	20,487
James E. Strunck	18,269
Catherine M. Richards	16,591
Donald Farrell Eslick	13,098

17TH DISTRICT—COOK COUNTY

Harold M. Nudelman	24,521
Frank Orlando	22,653
Harry Axelrod	4,774
Thomas E. Kramer	3,467
Write-ins	1

18TH DISTRICT—COOK COUNTY

Edward J. Rosewell	15,940
Leonard N. Foster	13,081
Edward L. Stepnowski	3,873
Howard A. Heldt	3,657
Write-ins	6

VOTE FOR MEMBERS OF THE CONSTITUTIONAL CONVENTION
GENERAL ELECTION—NOVEMBER 18, 1969—(Continued)

19TH DISTRICT—COOK COUNTY

Joseph C. Sharpe, Sr.	15,211
William A. Jaskula	14,655
Douglas Huff, Junior	2,625

20TH DISTRICT—COOK COUNTY

Victor A. Arrigo	15,515
Madison L. Brown	14,824
Write-ins	5

21ST DISTRICT—COOK COUNTY

Frank D. Stemberk	15,619
Gloria S. Pughsley	14,522
Joseph G. Policky	3,225

22ND DISTRICT—COOK COUNTY

James Kemp	17,546
Samuel A. Patch	17,345
Yolande M. Johnson	4,395
Write-ins	10

23RD DISTRICT—COOK COUNTY

Richard M. Daley	30,265
Leonard F. Miska	27,410
John P. Tully	5,275
Robert A. Urbanek	4,469
Write-ins	1

24TH DISTRICT—COOK COUNTY

Albert A. Raby	14,145
Odas Nicholson	12,330
Michael L. Shakman	11,707
Attye Belle McGee	9,205

25TH DISTRICT—COOK COUNTY

Francis X. Lawlor	25,387
Louis Marolda	16,311
Gabriel J. Barrett	15,769
Stanley A. Papierz	15,703

26TH DISTRICT—COOK COUNTY

Thomas E. Hunter	10,436
Clifford P. Kelley	10,108
Norman R. Robinson	3,586
Write-ins	3

27TH DISTRICT—COOK COUNTY

Michael J. Madigan	20,248
Joseph V. Rachunas	16,839
Joseph K. Prince	16,539
John J. Foy	15,270

28TH DISTRICT—COOK COUNTY

Ted A. Borek	16,046
Philip J. Carey	14,553
Edward P. Sheridan	14,110
Lendol D. Snow	13,711

29TH DISTRICT—COOK COUNTY

Charles A. Coleman	13,876
Richard K. Cooper	11,782
Mabry T. Roby, Jr.	5,421
Charles W. Cleveland	3,923
Write-ins	4

30TH DISTRICT—COOK COUNTY

David Linn	13,650
Mary Lee Leahy	12,460
Henry M. Soltysinski	12,306
John Chico	9,698
Write-ins	2

31ST DISTRICT—LAKE COUNTY

Mary A. Pappas	8,987
John D. Wenum	8,830
Glenn H. Reinier	8,650
Harold D. Wilson	4,651
Write-ins	6

32nd District

Counties	Jeannette Mullen	Jeffrey R. Ladd	Samuel T. Lawton, Jr.	Sheldon Karon	Write-ins
Lake	10,986	9,186	10,907	6,421	4
McHenry	5,645	7,268	4,617	4,591	
Total	16,631	16,454	15,524	11,012	4

VOTE FOR MEMBERS OF THE CONSTITUTIONAL CONVENTION
GENERAL ELECTION—NOVEMBER 18, 1969—(Continued)

33rd District

Counties	Stanley C. Johnson	Maxine Wymore	Jeff Strack	Earle B. Johnson	Write-ins
Boone	1,169	846	850	1,024	....
DeKalb	5,431	3,337	4,642	1,927	2
Kane	2,403	2,680	1,676	1,647	....
Kendall	589	437	195	273	....
McHenry	1,414	949	801	1,240	....
Winnebago	1,399	850	747	934	....
Total	12,405	9,099	8,911	7,045	2

34TH DISTRICT—WINNEBAGO COUNTY

Robert R. Canfield	11,753
Mrs. Thomas A. Keegan	11,304
John P. Graves, Jr.	7,471
Avery O. Gage	7,281

35th District

Counties	Harlan Rigney	Wayne W. Whalen	W. C. "Bill" Linker	Virginia Dare Matthews
Carroll	1,967	1,225	2,218	1,175
JoDaviess	1,581	2,265	1,076	554
Ogle	3,513	1,969	2,363	2,112
Stephenson	5,025	2,838	3,017	2,163
Whiteside	3,360	2,915	2,437	3,860
Total	15,446	11,212	11,111	9,864

36th District

Counties	Louis James Perona	Edwin F. Peterson	Arthur E. Quaife	James Lannon
Bureau	4,186	3,054	2,192	2,038
Henry	2,239	4,211	4,223	741
LaSalle	3,591	1,904	1,840	4,223
Lee	2,439	1,894	1,938	1,528
Total	12,455	11,063	10,193	8,530

37th District

Counties	Paul E. Mathias	David Davis	Richard G. Browne	Henry J. Spitzer	Write-ins
LaSalle	1,633	1,343	1,842	3,449	1
Livingston	3,225	2,467	1,710	2,102	....
McLean	6,145	6,393	6,295	2,226	....
Total	11,003	10,203	9,847	7,777	1

VOTE FOR MEMBERS OF THE CONSTITUTIONAL CONVENTION
GENERAL ELECTION—NOVEMBER 18, 1969—(Continued)

38th District

Counties	Betty (Mrs. Raymond) Howard	James S. Brannen	Albert N. Whitlock	Lawrence N. Hansen
Kane	16,186	11,754	10,956	9,458
Kendall	1,902	1,209	1,837	508
Total	18,088	12,963	12,793	9,966

39TH DISTRICT—DuPAGE COUNTY

Thomas C. Kelleghan	13,523
William A. Sommerschield	12,897
Stanley A. Kula	12,402
Margaret "Toni" Larson	12,203

40th District

Counties	Helen C. Kinney	Anthony M. Peccarelli	Helen S. Harshbarger	James H. Clark
DuPage	16,822	15,587	11,064	2,629
Will	1,869	911	3,589	816
Total	18,691	16,498	14,653	3,445

41st District

Counties	Louis F. Bottino	Arthur T. Lennon	George E. Sangmeister	Daniel L. Kennedy
Grundy	2,364	2,010	670	642
Will	9,452	9,693	9,191	7,757
Total	11,816	11,703	9,861	8,399

42nd District

Counties	John Linebaugh Knuppel	James S. Thompson	Ralph A. Killey	Troy A. Kost	Write-ins
Cass	1,229	893	542	399	
Fulton	3,030	1,996	848	2,274	
Knox	3,420	4,381	2,121	1,421	1
Mason	1,811	612	799	845	
Menard	1,891	931	705	290	
Peoria	775	570	230	322	
Warren	1,445	1,497	2,749	886	
Total	13,601	10,880	7,994	6,437	1

VOTE FOR MEMBERS OF THE CONSTITUTIONAL CONVENTION
GENERAL ELECTION—NOVEMBER 18, 1969—(Continued)

43rd District

Counties	Lewis D. Wilson	William R. Armstrong	Seymour P. Golden	Keith H. Johnson
Henderson	738	231	583	342
Mercer	1,402	955	743	1,057
Rock Island	9,900	8,729	7,258	6,497
Total	12,040	9,915	8,584	7,896

44th District

Counties	Charles R. Young	Edward H. Jenison	Joe T. Connelly	James Ray Livesay
Coles	1,311	1,545	2,845	4,035
Edgar	2,478	2,738	1,367	530
Vermilion	9,361	5,527	4,384	910
Total	13,150	9,810	8,596	5,475

45th District

Counties	John C. Parkhurst	David E. Connor	Victor J. Kasel	Joan R. Howells	Write-ins
Peoria	10,504	8,740	4,930	4,386	
Stark	569	530	260	212	18
Total	11,073	9,270	5,190	4,598	18

46th District

Counties	Donald D. Zeglis	Samuel L. Martin	Jack R. Beaupre	Mrs. Betty Lou Elliott
Champaign	751	1,126	446	436
Ford	1,178	1,612	732	439
Iroquois	1,816	4,230	1,269	1,611
Kankakee	8,531	2,982	6,642	5,406
Total	12,276	9,950	9,089	7,892

VOTE FOR MEMBERS OF THE CONSTITUTIONAL CONVENTION
GENERAL ELECTION—NOVEMBER 18, 1969—(Continued)
47th District

Counties	Charles W. Shuman	Henry I. Green	Joan Severns	John H. Finfrock
Champaign	5,473	7,882	6,001	4,314
DeWitt	1,442	1,049	832	360
Douglas	1,880	1,053	476	460
Moultrie	1,997	743	536	204
Piatt	1,500	1,421	503	447
Total	12,292	12,148	8,348	5,785

48th District

Counties	Clarence E. Yordy	William D. Fogal	Earl Madigan	John R. Lauer
Logan	1,765	812	3,911	4,143
Marshall	1,158	933	635	489
Putnam	385	327	340	198
Tazewell	6,898	8,335	3,340	2,187
Woodford	2,578	1,711	1,628	562
Total	12,784	12,118	9,854	7,579

49th District

Counties	Maurice W. Scott	William L. Fay	Thomas F. Londrigan	Walter L. Oblinger
Morgan	2,902	5,150	1,702	919
Sangamon	16,830	11,602	14,171	7,939
Total	19,732	16,752	15,873	8,858

50th District

Counties	Elbert S. Smith	Franklin E. Dove	W. A. (Art) Sappington	Marshall A. Susler
Christian	2,123	2,342	1,842	692
Macon	6,364	5,015	5,601	3,057
Shelby	1,824	2,856	1,194	370
Total	10,311	10,213	8,637	4,119

VOTE FOR MEMBERS OF THE CONSTITUTIONAL CONVENTION
GENERAL ELECTION—NOVEMBER 18, 1969—(Continued)

51st District

Counties	Dwight P. Friedrich	James S. Parker	C. F. Clem Marley	Walter Shipp
Bond.................................	734	551	455	475
Clinton...............................	2,161	1,253	673	753
Cumberland...........................	622	641	330	232
Effingham............................	2,468	2,938	1,588	915
Fayette...............................	1,541	1,292	1,331	902
Jasper................................	914	945	492	308
Marion................................	3,885	1,511	693	3,301
Montgomery...........................	1,726	1,597	3,548	1,184
Total.............................	14,051	10,728	9,110	8,070

52nd District

Counties	John Alexander	Stanley L. Klaus	Udell W. Wehling	Father Casimir F. Gierut
Calhoun...............................	366	676	537	305
Jersey................................	960	888	602	550
Macoupin.............................	5,015	5,297	2,475	3,800
Madison..............................	2,224	1,731	2,140	1,686
St. Clair.............................	1,602	1,411	1,439	661
Total.............................	10,167	10,003	7,193	7,002

53RD DISTRICT—MADISON COUNTY

Wendell Durr.........................	6,166
Ray Johnsen..........................	5,468
Doreen D. Young.....................	4,629
Lucien B. Ringering..................	3,609

54TH DISTRICT—ST. CLAIR COUNTY

John M. Karns, Jr.....................	6,375
William F. Fennoy, Jr.................	6,002
Charles "Chuck" Oelrich..............	4,496
Carolyn Chapman.....................	2,861
Lehman D. Krause (Write-in)..........	543

VOTE FOR MEMBERS OF THE CONSTITUTIONAL CONVENTION
GENERAL ELECTION—NOVEMBER 18, 1969—(Continued)
55th District

Counties	Henry Carter Hendren, Jr.	J. L. Buford	Parker Graves	Edgar E. Hall
Clark	675	1,018	690	507
Clay	888	1,175	605	949
Crawford	1,102	687	2,171	1,087
Edwards	2,184	1,436	244	294
Hamilton	680	674	258	440
Jefferson	1,778	2,314	1,151	2,249
Lawrence	870	898	1,019	476
Richland	935	1,064	580	391
Wabash	984	958	468	385
Wayne	1,940	1,671	459	764
Total	12,036	11,895	7,645	7,542

56th District

Counties	Ralph Dunn	David Kenney	Robert W. Holloway	Dean R. Hammack
Alexander	504	412	248	192
Jackson	2,323	2,908	1,669	888
Monroe	1,147	1,061	737	442
Perry	2,519	1,609	1,459	1,691
Randolph	1,837	1,493	2,322	1,488
St. Clair	758	601	494	259
Union	1,043	1,079	581	382
Washington	1,528	1,432	796	533
Total	11,659	10,595	8,306	5,875

57th District

Counties	Clifford L. Downen	Robert L. Butler	Bennie Cherry	H. B. Tanner
Franklin	2,282	1,990	3,394	815
Gallatin	531	366	723	477
Hardin	201	204	204	146
Johnson	534	519	287	289
Massac	548	474	120	158
Pope	429	463	91	122
Pulaski	683	574	369	189
Saline	1,122	1,115	1,072	1,518
White	1,067	901	710	706
Williamson	3,681	3,304	2,163	1,196
Total	11,078	9,910	9,133	5,616

**VOTE FOR MEMBERS OF THE CONSTITUTIONAL CONVENTION
GENERAL ELECTION—NOVEMBER 18, 1969—(Concluded)**

58th District

Counties	George J. Lewis	Matthew A. Hutmacher	Evelyn Sacadat	Theodore F. (Ted) Goehl	Write-ins
Adams	5,804	5,807	5,442	1,474	2
Brown	699	600	407	121	
Greene	926	790	476	180	
Hancock	1,773	1,441	1,240	332	
McDonough	1,740	1,351	1,245	324	
Pike	1,461	1,201	801	470	1
Schuyler	682	585	485	116	
Scott	565	483	336	126	
Total	13,650	12,258	10,432	3,143	3

Appendix D

SPECIAL ELECTION FOR THE
PROPOSED 1970 CONSTITUTION
DECEMBER 15, 1970

Summary of General Vote

Total number of electors voting at the election.. 2,017,717

Total number of votes cast on the following propositions:

Do you approve the proposed 1970 Constitution?
Number of Yes Votes... 1,122,425
Number of No Votes.. 838,168

Having been approved by a majority of the electors voting at the election, the 1970 proposed Constitution is, therefore, adopted.

1A. Election of the 177 members of the House of Representatives from multi-member districts by cumulative voting.
Number of Votes.. 1,031,241

Having been approved by a majority of the electors voting at the election, the proposition 1A is, therefore, adopted.

1B. Election of the 177 members of the House of Representatives from single member districts.
Number of Votes.. 749,909

Proposition 1B was not approved by a majority of the electors voting at the election, therefore, 1B was not adopted.

2A. The election by the voters of Judges nominated in primary elections or by petition.
Number of Votes.. 1,013,559

Having been approved by a majority of the electors voting at the election, the proposition 2A is, therefore, adopted.

2B. The appointment of Judges by the Governor from nominees submitted by Judicial Nominating Commissions.
Number of Votes.. 867,230

Proposition 2B was not approved by a majority of the electors voting at the election, therefore, 2B was not adopted.

Abolishing the death penalty.
Number of Yes Votes... 676,302
Number of No Votes.. 1,218,791

This proposition was not approved by a majority of the electors voting at the election, therefore, the proposition of abolishing the death penalty was not adopted.

Lowering the voting age to 18.
Number of Yes Votes... 869,816
Number of No Votes.. 1,052,924

This proposition was not approved by a majority of the electors voting at the election, therefore, the proposition of lowering the voting age to 18 was not adopted.

Source: Official Vote at General Election, November 3, 1970, pp. 102–104.

PROPOSED 1970 CONSTITUTION

County	Total Ballots Cast in the County	YES	%	NO	%
Adams	12,724	4,560	35.8	7,945	62.4
Alexander	1,552	393	25.3	1,090	70.2
Bond	2,568	513	20.0	1,981	77.1
Boone	4,103	1,748	42.6	2,321	56.6
Brown	1,250	486	38.9	734	58.7
Bureau	7,555	3,812	50.5	3,644	48.2
Calhoun	1,163	245	21.1	893	76.8
Carroll	3,317	2,089	63.0	1,179	35.5
Cass	2,726	1,153	42.3	1,520	55.8
Champaign	21,864	13,981	63.9	7,565	34.6
Christian	6,966	2,067	29.7	4,724	67.8
Clark	3,282	1,142	34.8	2,041	62.2
Clay	2,498	905	36.2	1,513	60.6
Clinton	5,064	777	15.3	4,187	82.7
Coles	9,219	2,816	30.5	6,290	68.2
Cook	(See below)				
Crawford	3,060	1,863	60.9	1,137	37.2
Cumberland	2,495	475	19.0	1,972	79.0
DeKalb	11,496	7,417	64.5	3,971	34.5
DeWitt	3,408	1,172	34.4	2,177	63.9
Douglas	3,737	1,391	37.2	2,289	61.3
DuPage	103,639	56,312	54.3	46,321	44.7
Edgar	4,908	1,552	31.6	3,197	65.1
Edwards	1,572	1,036	65.9	479	30.5
Effingham	5,786	1,904	32.9	3,669	63.4
Fayette	4,057	934	23.0	3,010	74.2
Ford	3,276	1,547	47.2	1,679	51.3
Franklin	6,616	1,549	23.4	4,848	73.3
Fulton	6,581	3,636	55.2	2,825	42.9
Gallatin	1,293	408	31.6	835	64.6
Greene	2,800	1,057	37.8	1,680	60.0
Grundy	5,379	1,882	35.0	3,421	63.6
Hamilton	2,053	381	18.6	1,594	77.6
Hancock	4,710	1,694	36.0	2,947	62.6
Hardin	760	103	13.6	624	82.1
Henderson	1,767	465	26.3	1,270	71.9
Henry	8,515	4,185	49.1	4,190	49.2
Iroquois	7,578	2,500	33.0	4,946	65.3
Jackson	7,161	4,660	65.1	2,254	31.5
Jasper	2,989	755	25.3	2,163	72.4
Jefferson	6,407	989	15.4	5,234	81.7
Jersey	3,354	613	18.3	2,563	76.4
JoDaviess	3,221	1,518	47.1	1,632	50.7
Johnson	1,188	547	46.0	577	48.6
Kane	42,534	24,472	57.5	18,061	42.5
Kankakee	17,824	5,340	30.0	12,106	67.9
Kendall	5,480	2,324	42.4	3,078	56.2
Knox	10,545	5,475	51.9	4,889	46.4
Lake	61,852	34,920	56.5	26,172	42.3
LaSalle	20,007	8,301	41.5	11,423	57.1
Lawrence	2,421	943	39.0	1,438	59.4
Lee	6,756	3,557	52.6	3,100	45.9
Livingston	6,936	3,469	50.0	3,307	47.7
Logan	6,532	2,480	38.0	3,949	60.5
McDonough	4,985	2,220	44.5	2,664	53.4

PROPOSED 1970 CONSTITUTION—(Concluded)

County	Total Ballots Cast in the County	YES	%	NO	%
McHenry	20,470	11,736	57.3	8,461	41.3
McLean	16,982	10,122	59.6	6,605	38.9
Macon	18,536	8,937	48.2	9,359	50.5
Macoupin	12,231	1,829	15.0	10,078	82.4
Madison	32,718	7,059	21.6	24,668	75.4
Marion	5,736	1,025	17.9	4,465	77.8
Marshall	2,709	1,532	56.6	1,131	41.7
Mason	3,155	1,793	56.8	1,310	41.5
Massac	1,402	688	49.1	642	45.8
Menard	2,339	979	41.9	1,318	56.3
Mercer	2,910	1,383	47.5	1,478	50.8
Monroe	3,106	1,136	36.6	1,897	61.1
Montgomery	9,141	1,140	12.5	7,755	84.8
Morgan	6,802	4,801	70.6	1,860	27.3
Moultrie	2,594	1,031	39.7	1,521	58.6
Ogle	7,880	3,601	45.7	4,160	52.8
Peoria	31,771	19,489	61.3	11,851	37.3
Perry	4,040	1,046	25.9	2,858	70.7
Piatt	3,286	1,124	34.2	2,108	64.2
Pike	3,769	1,447	38.4	2,241	59.5
Pope	798	208	26.1	559	70.1
Pulaski	1,149	424	36.9	660	57.4
Putnam	1,083	395	36.5	665	61.4
Randolph	4,840	1,959	40.5	2,760	57.0
Richland	2,705	686	25.4	1,953	72.2
Rock Island	19,534	10,963	56.1	8,269	42.3
St. Clair	31,733	5,840	18.4	24,721	77.9
Saline	4,236	1,775	41.9	2,226	52.5
Sangamon	35,555	14,417	40.5	20,282	57.0
Schuyler	1,726	477	27.6	1,209	70.0
Scott	1,336	724	54.2	577	43.2
Shelby	5,215	1,635	31.4	3,478	66.7
Stark	1,557	720	46.2	822	52.8
Stephenson	7,689	4,238	55.1	3,328	43.3
Tazewell	17,365	10,665	61.4	6,494	37.4
Union	2,321	1,203	51.8	1,037	44.7
Vermilion	16,835	6,065	36.0	10,505	62.4
Wabash	1,850	1,219	65.9	594	32.1
Warren	4,898	1,563	31.9	3,278	66.9
Washington	2,916	789	27.1	2,052	70.4
Wayne	3,272	668	20.4	2,534	77.4
White	3,128	1,260	40.3	1,777	56.8
Whiteside	8,283	4,964	59.9	3,219	38.9
Will	39,041	17,505	44.8	21,000	53.8
Williamson	6,378	2,820	44.2	3,340	52.4
Winnebago	35,321	15,501	43.9	19,328	54.7
Woodford	5,355	3,085	57.6	2,175	40.6
Down State	949,225	426,399	44.9	505,926	53.3
Cook County	1,068,492	696,026	65.1	332,242	31.1
Total	2,017,717	1,122,425	55.6	838,168	41.5

Index

AFL–CIO: opposition to convention call, 33, 34; opposition to new constitution, 81–82; support for eighteen-year-old vote, 97

Alexander, John, 69

Allen, William: early involvement in constitutional reform, 9; campaign manager of ratification effort, 72; on Daley endorsement, 76; on funding for ratification, 78

Ancel, Louis, 14

Arrington, Senator Russell: withdraws as delegate candidate, 48–49

Bane, Charles, 14

Bergstrom, Robert, 14

Block, Joseph, 16

Blue ballot: history and object of, 17–18; public and, 27; "vote 'yes' on the Blue Ballot," 30–31. See also Convention call election

Burger, Chief Justice Warren: on merit selection, 93

Carlson, Mrs. Elmer, 14

Chamber of Commerce, 14; and nonpartisan delegate election, 45; on proposed constitution, 79

Chicago Bar Association: support for convention call, 13, 25, 35; and nonpartisan delegate election, 45; on proposed constitution, 79

Citizens for Single-Member Districts, 89–90

City Club of Chicago, 14

Cohn, Rubin, 91

Colorado: merit selection campaign in, 92

Commercial Club: and convention call campaign, 24

Commission on Urban Area Government, 80

Committee for Better Courts in Illinois, 91–92

Committee for Modern Courts, 91

Committee to Oppose a Con Con in Illinois, 33

Consensualism: and constitutional issues, 5–7. See also Nonvoter; Voter participation

Constitution: underlying support for, 72

Constitutional Committee Information Service, 14, 15, 25

Constitutional Convention: legislative call for, 11–12

Constitutional propositions: history of voting on, 19–20

Constitution Study Commission: creation of, 10–11

Convention call campaign: cochairmen of, 9, 15–16; developing strategy for, 23–24; financing, 24–26; local citizens' committees, 26–27; themes, 27–32; literature, 32–34; opposition, 33–34

Convention call election: ballot controversy, 17–22; participation in, 36; and federal election, 37–38; pattern of results, 40–42; methods and results, 42

Cook County: vote on ratification, 99–100; vote on separate issues, 102

Cook County Democratic party:
effect on death penalty vote, 96;
and ratification vote, 100
Coordinating Committee to Defeat
the Proposed Constitution, 81
Counties: in proposed constitution, 72
Cumulative voting, 65; labor
attitude toward, 82; black
support for, 82; as campaign
issue, 89–90. *See also* Legislative
representation

Daley, Mayor Richard: and nonpartisan delegate elections, 46;
and ballot position controversy,
50; endorses proposed constitution, 75–76; boycotts signing
ceremony, 83; effect of endorsement, 85; endorses propositions
1–A and 2–A, 93–94
Death penalty: strategy of campaign to abolish, 95–96; ratification vote on, 96, 106–108
Delegate election, 12; partisan vs.
nonpartisan, 43–46, 58–61;
ballot position, 49–54; factors
contributing to success, 55–57;
campaign styles, 57–58; voter
participation, 62–63
Delegate nomination, 46–49
Delegates: profiles of candidates,
61–63; and ratification
campaign, 76–77
Democratic party: and new constitution, 82–85; split on judicial
selection, 94; and ratification,
105
Dixon, Alan J.: on taxpayers and
proposed constitution, 77
Douglass, Kingman, Jr., 24, 26–
27; cochairman of convention
call committee, 16; and nonpartisan delegate election, 45
Dreiske, John: on Arrington withdrawal, 49; editorial on Democratic strategy, 84

Ed, Don, 51
Eighteen-year-old vote: campaign
for, 97–98; ratification vote on,
98, 106–108

Elward, Paul: on delegate represen-
tativeness, 13–14; opposes constitution, 84

Gateway amendment, 8; and blue
ballot, 17–18
Gertz, Elmer, 95–96
Goldberg, Arthur: on merit selec-
tion, 93
Governor: and convention call co-
chairmen, 15–16. *See also*
Kerner, Governor Otto; Ogilvie,
Governor Richard; Shapiro,
Governor Samuel

Hacker, Andrew, 77–78
Hanahan, Thomas, 12–13
Hendren, Henry, 76
Home rule: and ratification cam-
paign, 80
House of Representatives. *See*
Cumulative voting
Howlett, Michael: and nonparti-
san delegate selection, 45

Illinois Agricultural Association,
14, 16; and nonpartisan delegate
selection, 45
Illinois Citizens for a New Constitution, 71–79, 88
Illinois Committee for a Constitutional Convention, 16, 23–25
Illinois Committee for Constitutional Revision, 9, 14
Illinois Congress of Parents and
Teachers, 14; and convention
call campaign, 26; and proposed
constitution, 79
Illinois Education Association, 14;
and proposed constitution, 75,
79
Illinois Municipal League, 14; and
proposed constitution, 79, 80
Income tax: state, 78, 87
Independent Voters of Illinois: and
merit selection campaign, 93

Jackson, Reverend Jesse, 93;
supports merit selection, 94
Judicial selection, 66; 1958 reforms,
9; and ratification campaign,
91–95; vote results, 94, 106–108;
downstate campaign, 94

Katz, Harold: party-circle ballot plan, 18–20; and delegate selection, 44

Keegan, Betty Ann: amendment on separate submissions, 68

Kerner, Governor Otto: support for constitutional convention, 11; and financing of convention call campaign, 25

Kitsos, Thomas: on constitutional amendment voters, 4–41

Kuthfuss, William J.: cochairman of convention call committee, 16

Labor: opposition to new constitution, 81–82; and death penalty vote, 96

Larsen, Verna, 14

League of Women Voters: and convention call, 13, 26; on proposed constitution, 79

Leahy, Mary Lee: and suit on ballot position controversy, 51–53

Legislative representation: and ratification campaign, 88–90; ratification vote on, 106–108. *See also* Cumulative voting

Lewis, John W., 12, 45

Local government: in new constitution, 72–80

Lockhart, Richard: early involvement in constitutional reform, 9

Lyons, Thomas, 45

McGloon, Thomas, 45

Murtaugh, Timothy III, 14

NAACP: opposition to new constitution, 82

Nonvoter: profile, 108–115; attitudes toward separate issues, 112; reasons for nonparticipation, 113–114

Norton, Peggy, 14

Ogilvie, Governor Richard: endorses proposed constitution, 71; telegram to Republican county chairmen, 85–86; on merit selection, 93

Operation Breadbasket, 82; and merit selection campaign, 93

Otis, James T., 14, 48

Party-circle ballot, 18–19

Pebworth, Marjorie, 10; death of, 12

Pollution control: as part of proposed constitution, 72

Powell, Secretary of State Paul: and ballot position controversy, 50–54

PTA. *See* Illinois Congress of Parents and Teachers

Ratification: minimal turnout strategy, 5, 114; and issue of separate submissions, 65–66; funding for campaign, 74–75; revenue issue and, 77–79; and state income tax, 78; election results, 99–102; vote on separate issues, 102–103; urban-rural vote, 103; voter profile, 103–108; profile of nonvoter, 108–115; reasons for nonparticipation, 113–114

Reagan, Ronald: on merit selection, 93

Referendum: choice of date for, 69. *See also* Ratification

Republican party: endorses constitution, 83, 85–86; and ratification, 105

Revenue issue: opponents and, 77, 81

Robertson, Mary Helen, 14

Sandquist, Elroy C. Jr., 14

Save Our State committees, 33, 75, 81

Scott, William: on revenue article and ratification, 77

Senate Joint Resolution 2: approval of, 11–12

Separate submissions, 65–66; campaign for, 87–98; votes on, 102–103; voting patterns on, 106–108; nonvoter opinions on, 108–115

Shapiro, Governor Samuel: and Blue Ballot Week, 35

Simon, Paul: on party-circle ballot, 18; and nonpartisan delegate selection, 45; support for merit selection, 94

Small Businessman's Association: opposed to new constitution, 80
Smith, Ralph T., 45
Social justice: as aspect of proposed constitution, 72
Sommerschield, William, 88
SOS. *See* Save Our State committees
Stevenson, Adlai E. III; and fund raising for convention call campaign, 25; and delegate selection, 45; on merit selection, 93–94
Stoneking, Wayne, 14

Tomei, Peter, 14; and nonpartisan delegate election, 45

United Auto Workers: favor convention call, 34; endorses constitution, 81; contribution to eighteen-year-old vote campaign, 98

Voter participation, 5–6; on constitutional propositions, 11; on convention call, 21–22; related to awareness of Con Con, 29; in convention call election, 36; tendency profile of nonparticipant, 39–40; and results of convention call election, 41–42; and delegate election, 62–63; in ratification election, 99, 108–115. *See also* Blue Ballot; Nonvoter

Wallace, George: presidential campaign and convention call, 37–38
Weisberg, Bernard: and suit in ballot position controversy, 51–52
Whalen, Wayne: on separate submissions, 68; and merit selection, 91
Wilson, Lewis: on separate submissions, 68
Witwer, Samuel, 14; early involvement in constitutional reform, 8–9; role in choosing convention call cochairmen, 16; on party-circle ballot, 21; on separate submissions, 67

FROM THE SERIES

Studies in Illinois Constitution Making
EDITED BY JOSEPH P. PISCIOTTE

ELECTING A CONSTITUTION
The Illinois Citizen and the 1970 Constitution
JoAnna M. Watson

From her vantage point as journalist and as participant-observer in the campaign for a new Illinois constitution, JoAnna M. Watson gained a unique insight into the behind-the-scenes maneuverings of the ratification process. She was a firsthand witness to the major catalysts for creation of the new constitution: the long-term involvement of a group of reform-minded citizens; strong support — dating back to the 1950 Gateway amendment — for blue ballot propositions; the recognition that, with half of Illinois' population concentrated in one northern county, a balancing of electoral forces was necessary; and the public's awareness of the persistent diligence of convention delegates.

Taking us through each stage of the constitutional revision process, Watson analyzes the campaigns leading to four separate statewide elections and focuses on: the call for a convention, the primaries and general election of convention delegates, and finally the ratification election on December 15, 1970. Watson emphasizes that the ultimate success of this lengthy process required a variety of strategies, not only at different points in the process itself, but also in the various geographic regions of Illinois. Thus, while the successful referendum election in November 1968 was based simply on the concept of "modernization," the final ratification campaign included both individual delegate efforts in selected areas and the typical precinct level, get-out-the-vote approach in Cook County. Taken together, these campaigns made for a strategy of success that will be useful and fascinating to students of Illinois politics, as well as to citizens interested in the history of their state.

JOANNA M. WATSON is director of summer school and community education at Mercer University in Macon, Georgia.

UNIVERSITY OF ILLINOIS PRESS *Urbana   Chicago   London*

ISBN 0-252-00458-2